Nick Vandome

iPad
for Seniors

3rd edition covers iOS 7
for iPad 2 – 5 (iPad Air) and iPad Mini

In easy steps is an imprint of In Easy Steps Limited
16 Hamilton Terrace · Holly Walk · Leamington Spa
Warwickshire · United Kingdom · CV32 4LY
www.ineasysteps.com

Third Edition

Notice of Liability
Every effort has been made to ensure that this book contains accurate
and current information. However, In Easy Steps Limited and the
author shall not be liable for any loss or damage suffered by readers
as a result of any information contained herein.

Trademarks
iPad® is a registered trademark of Apple Computer, Inc. All other
trademarks are acknowledged as belonging to their respective
companies.

In Easy Steps Limited supports The Forest Stewardship Council (FSC),
the leading international forest certification organization. All our titles
that are printed on Greenpeace approved FSC certified paper carry the
FSC logo.

MIX
Paper from
responsible sources
FSC® C020837

Printed and bound in the United Kingdom

ISBN 978-1-84078-610-1

Contents

1 Choosing your iPad 7

The iEverything	8
Simplicity of the iPad	9
iPad or iPad Mini?	10
Specifications Explained	11
Before you Switch On	12
Getting Started	13
About iOS 7	14
Home Screen	15
Home Button	16
Opening Items	17
Charging your iPad	18

2 Around your iPad 19

iPad Settings	20
Using the Dock	22
Multitasking Window	24
Closing Items	25
Using the Control Center	26
Navigating Around	28
Swipe, Tap and Pinch	29
Finding Things with Siri	32
Searching with Spotlight	34
Living in the iCloud	35
Updating Software	38
Using the Lock Screen	39
iPad Smart Cover	40
Accessibility Issues	41

3 The iPad Keyboard 47

It's Virtually a Keyboard	48
Keyboard Settings	50

Entering Text   52
Editing Text   53
Moving the Keyboard   55
Keyboard Shortcuts   57
Voice Typing   60

4 Knowing your Apps   61

What is an App?   62
Built-in Apps   63
About the App Store   66
Finding Apps   68
Downloading Apps   72
Updating Apps   73
Organizing Apps   74
Deleting Apps   76

5 Keeping in Touch   77

Getting Online   78
Obtaining an Apple ID   79
Setting up an Email Account   80
Emailing   82
Adding Social Networking   85
Having a Video Chat   86
Messaging   88
Phoning with Skype   90
Communication Apps   92

6 On a Web Safari   93

Around Safari   94
Safari Settings   96
Navigating Pages   98
Opening New Tabs   99
Bookmarking Pages   100
Reading List and Shared Links   101
Web Apps   102

7 Staying Organized 103

Taking Notes	104
Setting Reminders	106
Using the Calendar	108
Your iPad Address Book	110
Keeping Notified	111
Viewing Notifications	112
Do Not Disturb	113
Organization Apps	114
Productivity Apps	115
Saving Documents	116
Printing Items	118

8 Like a Good Book 119

Newspapers and Magazines	120
Finding Books	122
Reading Books	126
Kindle on your iPad	130

9 Leisure Time 133

Buying Music	134
Playing Music	135
Using the Camera	136
Viewing Photos	138
Creating Albums	140
Selecting Photos	141
Sharing Photos	142
Editing Photos	144
In the Photo Booth	146
Capturing Videos	147
Viewing Videos	148
Photo and Video Apps	149
Discovering Art	150
Creating Pictures	151
Cooking with your iPad	152

Staying Healthy 153
Playing Games 154

10 Getting on the Map 155

Looking Around Maps 156
Finding Locations 158
Using Pins 159
Getting Directions 160
Finding Contacts 163
Types of Maps 164
Using Flyover 165

11 Traveling Companion 167

Traveling with your iPad 168
Planning your Trip 169
Viewing Flights 171
Finding Hotels 172
Converting Currency 173
Travel Apps 174

12 Practical Matters 177

Setting Restrictions 178
Finding your iPad 180
Locking your iPad 182
Avoiding Viruses 183
Dealing with Money 184
Looking at Property 185
Financial Apps 186

Index 187

1 Choosing your iPad

It's compact, it's stylish, it's powerful, and it's perfect for anyone, of any age. This chapter introduces the iPad and its iOS 7 operating system so you can quickly get up and running with this exciting tablet.

8 The iEverything

9 Simplicity of the iPad

10 iPad or iPad Mini?

11 Specifications Explained

12 Before you Switch On

13 Getting Started

14 About iOS 7

15 Home Screen

16 Home Button

17 Opening Items

18 Charging your iPad

The iEverything

The iPad is a tablet computer that has gone a long way to change how we think of computers and how we interact with them. Instead of a large, static object it is effortlessly mobile and even makes a laptop seem bulky by comparison.

But even with its compact size, the iPad still manages to pack a lot of power and functionality into its diminutive body. In this case, small is very definitely beautiful and the range of what you can do with the iPad is considerable:

- Communicate via email, video and text messaging.

- Surf the Web wirelessly.

- Add an endless number of new 'apps' from the Apple App Store.

- Use a range of entertainment tools, covering music, photos, video, books and games.

- Do all of your favorite productivity tasks such as word processing, creating spreadsheets or producing presentations.

- Organize your life with apps for calendars, address books, notes, reminders and much more.

'Apps' is just a fancy name for what are more traditionally called programs in the world of computing. The iPad has several apps that come built-in and ready for use. There are thousands more available for downloading from the online App Store (see Chapter Four, page 66).

The New icon pictured above indicates a new or enhanced feature introduced with the latest version of iOS 7.

Add to this up to 10 hours' battery life when you are on the move, two different sizes (with a Retina Display screen of outstanding clarity) and a seamless backup system, and it is clear why the iPad can stylishly fulfil all of your computing needs.

Simplicity of the iPad

Computers have become a central part of our everyday lives, but there is no reason why they need to be complex devices that have us scratching our heads as to how to best use them. The iPad is not only stylish and compact, it also makes the computing process as simple as possible, so you can concentrate on what you want to do. Some ways in which this is done are:

- **Instantly on.** With the iPad there is no long wait for it to turn on, or wake from a state of sleep. When you turn it on, it is ready to use, it's as simple as that.

- **Apps.** iPad apps sit on the Home screen, visible and ready to use. Most apps are created in a similar format, so once you have mastered getting around them you will be comfortable using most apps.

- **Settings.** One of the built-in iPad apps is for Settings. This is a one-stop shop for customizing the way that your iPad looks and operates and also how settings for apps work.

- **Dock and Multitasking.** These are two functions that enable you to access your favorite apps quickly, regardless of what you are doing on your iPad.

- **Home button.** This enables you to return to the main Home screen at any time. It also has some additional functionality, depending on how many times you click it.

Hot tip

Much of the way you navigate around the iPad is done by tapping, or swiping, with your fingers, rather than with a traditional keyboard and mouse. There is also a virtual keyboard for input functions.

Don't forget

The Dock is the bar at the bottom of the iPad screen, onto which apps can be placed for quick access.

iPad or iPad Mini?

Since its introduction in 2010 the iPad has evolved in both its size and specifications. When choosing your iPad the first consideration is which size to select. There are two options:

- **Full size iPad.** This is the original size of the iPad. It measures 9.7 inches (diagonal) and has a high resolution Retina Display screen.

- **iPad Mini.** The iPad Mini is similar in most respects to the larger version, except for its size. The screen measures 7.9 inches (diagonal) and is also lighter than the full size version.

iOS 7 can be used on all iPads from the iPad 2 onwards and all versions of the iPad Mini.

iPad
with Retina display

iPad mini

The full size iPad not only currently has a higher resolution screen, it also has a slightly faster processor and some versions have larger storage capacities. However, in terms of functionality there is not a great difference between the two and the choice may depend on the size of screen that you prefer and how portable you would like your iPad to be (both versions are highly portable but the iPad Mini fits in a smaller pocket or bag).

Another variation in the iPad family is how they connect to the Internet and online services. There are two options:

- **With Wi-Fi connectivity.** This enables you to connect to the Internet via a Wi-Fi router, either in your own home, or at a Wi-Fi hotspot.

- **With Wi-Fi and 4G connectivity (where available, but it also covers 3G).** This should be considered if you will need to connect to the Internet when you are traveling away from home with a cellular connection.

4G and 3G enables you to connect to a mobile network to access the Internet, in the same way as with a cell/mobile phone. This requires a contract with a provider of this service, usually one of the cell/mobile phone companies.

Specifications Explained

When choosing your iPad some of the specifications to consider are:

- **Processor:** This determines the speed at which the iPad operates and how quickly tasks are performed.

- **Storage:** This determines how much content you can store on your iPad. Across the iPad family, the range of storage is 16GB, 32GB, 64GB or 128GB.

- **Connectivity:** The options for this are Wi-Fi and 3G/4G connectivity for the Internet, and Bluetooth for connecting to other devices over short distances.

- **Screen:** Look for an iPad with a Retina Display screen for the highest resolution and best clarity. This is an LED-backlit screen and available on the latest iPads.

- **Operating System**. The full size version of the iPad and the iPad Mini both run on the iOS 7 operating system.

- **Battery power:** This is the length of time the iPad can be used for general use such as surfing the Web on Wi-Fi, watching video, or listening to music. All models offer approximately 10 hours of use in this way.

- **Input/Output:** Both the iPad and the iPad Mini have similar output/input options. These are a lightning connector port (for charging), 3.5 mm stereo headphone minijack, built-in speaker, microphone and micro-SIM card tray (Wi-Fi and 4G model only).

- **Sensors:** These are used to access the amount of ambient light and also the orientation in which the iPad is being held. The sensors are accelerometer, ambient light sensor and gyroscope.

- **TV and video:** This determines how your iPad can be connected to a High Definition TV. This is done with AirPlay Mirroring.

The amount of storage you need may change once you have bought your iPad. If possible, buy a version with as much as possible.

Both the iPad and iPad Mini have an iSight camera on the back, which can take high resolution photos and capture video in high definition.

To connect your iPad to an HDTV you will need an Apple Lightning (or Dock) Digital AV Adapter or an Apple Lightning (or Dock) to VGA Adapter (sold separately).

Before you Switch On

The external controls for the iPad are simple. Three of them are situated at the top of the iPad and the other is in the middle at the bottom. There are also two cameras, one on the front and one on the back of the iPad.

Controls

The controls at the top of the iPad are:

On/Off button

Side switch for silent mode (this applies to system sounds rather than the volume of items such as music or videos)

Volume Up or **Down** button

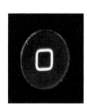

Cameras. One is located on the back, underneath the On/Off button and one on the front, top

Home button. Press this once to wake up the iPad or return to the Home screen at any point:

Speaker. The speaker is located on the bottom of the iPad:

Lightning connector. Connect the Lightning connector here to charge the iPad, or connect it to another computer. (See page 18 for more information on the connector for previous versions of the iPad)

Getting Started

To start using the iPad, press the On/Off button once and hold it down for a few seconds.

Initially there will be a series of Setup screens to move through before you can use the iPad. These include the following options (a lot of these can be skipped during the Setup and accessed later from the **Settings** app):

- **Language.** Select the language you want to use.

- **Country.** Select the country in which you are located.

- **Location Services.** This determines whether your iPad can use your geographical location for apps that use this type of information (such as Maps).

- **Wi-Fi network.** Select a Wi-Fi network to connect to the Internet. If you are at home, this will be your own Wi-Fi network, if available. If you are at a Wi-Fi hotspot then this will appear on your network list.

- **Apple ID.** You can register with this to be able to access a range of Apple facilities, such as iCloud, purchase items on iTunes or the App Store, Facetime, Messages and iBooks. You can also create an Apple ID whenever you access one of the relevant apps for the first time.

- **iCloud.** This is Apple's online service for sharing and backing up content. See Chapter Two for details.

- **Find My iPad.** This is a service that can be activated so that you can locate your iPad if it is lost or stolen. This is done via the online iCloud site at **www.icloud.com**

- **Diagnostic information.** This enables information about your iPad to be sent to Apple.

- **Register.** This enables you to register your iPad with Apple, as the registered owner.

- **Start using.** Once the Setup process has been completed you can start using your iPad.

For details about obtaining an Apple ID see Chapter Five.

For more information about using iCloud see Chapter Two.

The Find My iPad function can also be set up within the **Privacy > Location Services** and **iCloud** sections of the **Settings** app (see page 180).

About iOS 7

iOS 7 is the latest version of the operating system for Apple's mobile devices including the iPad, the iPhone and the iPod Touch.

iOS 7 is one of the most dramatic cosmetic changes to the operating system in its history. It was overseen by the designer Jonathan Ive, who was responsible for some of the most iconic Apple devices including the iMac, iPod and iPhone. The design is intended to be a cleaner, simpler one for the icons and apps and moves away from previous styles, which relied on the interpretation of everyday materials such as paper, leather, wood and felt.

The interpretation of everyday items in the design of computer interfaces is known as skeuomorphic.

iOS 7 icons	iOS 6 icons

iOS 7 is designed to be as visually appealing as possible and one way in which this is done is to produce the effect of different layers for the elements of the operating system. For instance, when you are viewing the Home screen, the layer with the apps appears to move independently from the background when you tilt and move the iPad. Also, a specific color palette has been used across all of the built-in apps to give as much consistency as possible.

To check the version of the iOS, look in **Settings > General > Software Update**.

The operation of iOS 7 is generally the same as for previous versions of the operating system but the design has helped to take the experience for the user to a new level.

Home Screen

Once you have completed the Setup process you will see the Home screen of the iPad. This contains the built-in apps:

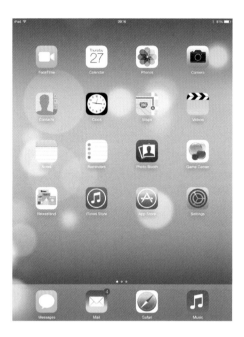

At the bottom of the screen are four apps that appear by default in the Dock area.

Rotate the iPad and the orientation changes automatically.

There are 34 different wallpaper backgrounds for iOS 7 on the iPad. These can be found in **Settings > Wallpapers & Brightness**. Some of the wallpapers are **Dynamic**, which means that they appear to move independently from the apps icons when you tilt the iPad. The other backgrounds are **Stills** and you can also use your own pictures from the Photos app. The examples used in this book are from the dynamic range.

Items on the Dock can be removed and new ones can be added. For more details see Chapter Two.

Home Button

The Home button, located at the bottom, middle on the iPad, can be used to perform a number of tasks:

1 Click once on the **Home** button to return to the Home screen at any point

2 Double-click on the **Home** button to access the **Multitasking** window. This shows the most recently-used and open apps

3 Press and hold on the **Home** button to access the Siri voice assistant function

For more information about using the iPad search facilities, see Chapter Two.

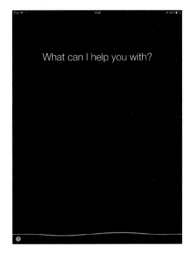

What can I help you with?

Opening Items

All apps on your iPad can be opened with the minimum of fuss and effort:

1 Tap once on an icon to open the app

2 The app opens at its Home screen

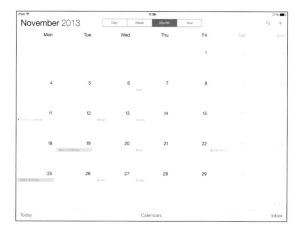

For details about closing items see Chapter Two.

3 Click once on the **Home** button to return to the Home screen

4 From the Multitasking window swipe between apps and tap on one to open it directly

Charging your iPad

The iPad comes with a Lightning connector to USB Cable and a USB Power Adapter, for charging the iPad:

Previous versions of the iPad have a Dock connector, with 30 pins, instead of a Lightning connector, which only has 8 pins.

1 Connect the USB end of the Lightning connector to the Power Adapter

If you have older accessories with Dock connector points you can buy a Lightning to 30-pin adapter so that you can still use them with a fourth generation (and later) iPad.

2 Connect the other end of the Lightning connector to the iPad

3 Plug in the Power Adapter

The iPad can also be charged by connecting it with the Lightning connector to another computer. However, this has to be another Mac computer and, if it is a MacBook, it also has to be plugged in for the iPad to charge.

2 Around your iPad

Once you have turned on your iPad you will want to start using it as soon as possible. This chapter shows how to do this with details about settings, navigation, accessibility features, the voice assistant Siri and also registering for and setting up the iCloud service for sharing your content.

20 iPad Settings

22 Using the Dock

24 Multitasking Window

25 Closing Items

26 Using the Control Center

28 Navigating Around

29 Swipe, Tap and Pinch

32 Finding Things with Siri

34 Searching with Spotlight

35 Living in the iCloud

38 Updating Software

39 Using the Lock Screen

40 iPad Smart Cover

41 Accessibility Issues

iPad Settings

The Settings app is the one that should probably be explored first as it controls settings for the appearance of the iPad and the way it, and its apps, operate. To use the Settings app:

Don't forget

If a Settings option has an On/Off button next to it, this can be changed by swiping the button to either the left or right. Green indicates that the option is **On**.

1 The Settings are listed down the left-hand side and the options are shown on the right-hand side

2 Tap on a link to see additional options for that item

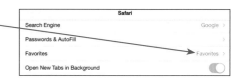

Don't forget

If you have an iPad with 3G/4G connectivity then there will also be a setting for Cellular.

The System Settings are:

- **Airplane Mode.** This can be used while on an airplane.

- **Wi-Fi.** This enables you to select a wireless network.

- **Bluetooth.** Turn this On to connect Bluetooth devices.

- **Notification Center.** This determines how the Notification Center operates (see Chapter Seven).

- **Control Center.** This determines how the Control Center operates (see pages 26-27).

- **Do Not Disturb.** Use this to specify times when you do not want to receive audio alerts or FaceTime video calls.

- **General.** This contains a number of options for how the iPad operates. This is one of the most useful Settings.

- **Sounds.** This has options for setting sounds for alerts.

- **Brightness & Wallpaper.** This can be used to set the screen brightness and select a wallpaper.

- **Privacy.** This can be used to activate Location Services so that your location can be used by specific apps.

- **iCloud.** This contains settings for items that are to be saved to the online iCloud.

- **Mail, Contacts, Calendars.** This has options for how these three apps operate.

- **Notes.** This contains formatting options for creating items in the Notes app.

- **Reminders.** This has an option for syncing your reminders for other devices, covering a period of time.

- **Messages.** This can be used to sign in to the Messages app for sending and receiving text messages.

- **FaceTime.** This is used to turn video calling On or Off.

- **Maps.** This contains options for displaying distances and the default method for displaying directions.

- **Safari.** Settings for the Safari web browser.

- **iTunes & App Stores.** This can be used to specify downloading options for the iTunes and App Stores.

- **Music.** This has options for how you listen to music.

- **Videos.** This has options for how you view videos.

- **Photos & Camera.** This has options for viewing and editing photos, slideshow settings and options for uploading to iCloud, and using Shared Photo Streams.

- **iBooks.** This contains options for reading books in the iBooks app, including hyphenation and using bookmarks.

- **Newsstand.** Use this set of options to automatically download new content for items in the Newsstand app.

To change the iPad's wallpaper, tap once on the arrow next to the iPad icon in the **Brightness & Wallpaper** Setting. From here you can select system images, or ones that you have taken yourself and saved on your iPad.

Tap once here to move back to the previous page for the selected Setting:

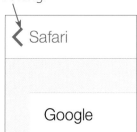

21

Using the Dock

By default, there are four apps on the Dock at the bottom of the screen. These are the four that Apple thinks you will use most frequently:

- Messaging, for text messages

- Mail, for email

- Safari, for web browsing

- Music

You can rearrange the order in which the Dock apps appear:

Hot tip

Just above the Dock is a line of small white dots. These indicate how many screens of content there are on the iPad. Tap on one of the dots to go to that screen.

1 Tap and hold on one of the Dock apps until it starts to jiggle

2 Drag the app into its new position

3 Click once on the **Home** button to return from edit mode

Adding and removing Dock apps

You can also remove apps from the Dock and add new ones:

1 To remove an app from the Dock, tap and hold it and drag it onto the main screen area

2 To add an app to the Dock, tap and hold it and drag it onto the Dock

If items are removed from the Dock they are still available in the same way from the main screen.

3 The number of items that can be added to the Dock is restricted to a maximum of six as the icons do not resize themselves

4 Click once on the **Home** button to return from edit mode

Multitasking Window

The Multitasking feature has been overhauled in iOS 7 and it performs a number of tasks:

- It shows open apps

- It enables you to move between open apps and open different ones

- It enables apps to be closed (see next page)

Accessing Multitasking
The Multitasking option can be accessed from any screen on your iPad, as follows:

1 Double-click on the **Home** button

2 The currently-open apps are displayed, with their icons underneath them (except the Home screen). The most recently-used apps are shown first

3 Swipe left and right to view the open apps. Tap on one to access it in full screen size

Closing Items

The iPad deals with open apps very efficiently. They do not interact with other apps, which increases security and also means that they can be open in the background, without using up a significant amount of processing power, in a state of semi-hibernation until they are needed. Because of this it is not essential to close apps when you move to something else. However, you may want to close apps if you feel you have too many open or if one stops working. To do this:

1 Access the Multitasking window. The currently-open apps are displayed

2 Press and hold on an app and swipe it to the top of the screen to close it. This does not remove it from the iPad and it can be opened again in the usual way

3 The app is removed from its position in the Multitasking window

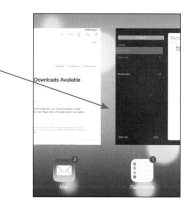

When you switch from one app to another, the first one stays open in the background. You can go back to it by accessing it from the Multitasking window or the Home screen.

Beware

The Control Center cannot be disabled from being accessed from the Home screen.

Using the Control Center

The Control Center is a panel containing some of the most commonly used options within the **Settings** app. It can be accessed with one swipe and is an excellent function for when you do not want to have to go into Settings.

Accessing the Control Center

The Control Center can be accessed from any screen within iOS 7 and it can also be accessed from the Lock Screen:

1 Tap once on the **Settings** app

2 Tap once on the **Control Center** tab and drag the

Access on Lock Screen and **Access Within Apps** buttons On or Off to specify if the Control Center can be accessed from there (if both are Off, it can still be accessed from any Home screen)

3 Swipe up from the bottom of any screen to access the Control Center panel

4 Tap on this button to hide the Control Center panel, or tap anywhere on the screen

Control Center controls

The items that can be used in the Control Center are:

1 Use these controls for any music or video that is playing. Use the buttons to Pause/Play a track, go to the beginning or end and adjust the volume

2 Tap once on this button to turn **Airplane mode** On or Off

3 Tap once on this button to turn **Wi-Fi** On or Off

4 Tap once on this button to turn **Bluetooth** On or Off

5 Tap once on this button to turn **Do Not Disturb** mode On or Off

6 Tap once on this button to access a clock, including a stopwatch

7 Tap once on this button to open the **Camera** app

8 Use this slider to adjust the screen brightness

9 Tap once on this button to **Lock** or **Unlock** screen rotation. If it is locked, the screen will not change when you change the orientation of your iPad

Hot tip

The screen rotation can also be locked from within the **General** section of the **Settings** app. Under **Use Side Switch to**, tap once on the **Lock Rotation** link. Then the side switch can be used to lock, and unlock, the screen rotation.

Multitasking Gestures and Multitouch Gestures are the same and the terms are interchangeable.

You can also move between different screens by tapping once on the small white dots in the middle of the screen above the Dock.

You can also return to the Home screen by clicking once on the Home button.

Navigating Around

Most of the navigation on the iPad is done with Multitasking Gestures, which are looked at on the next three pages. Two of these can also be used for basic navigation:

Swiping between screens
Once you have added more apps to your iPad they will start to fill up more screens. To move between these:

Swipe left or right with one or two fingers.

Returning to the Home screen
Pinch together with thumb and four fingers to return to the Home screen from any open app.

Swipe, Tap and Pinch

Since there is no mouse connected to the iPad, navigation is done with your fingers. There is a combination of tapping, swiping and pinching gestures that can be used to view items such as web pages, photos, maps and documents and also navigate around the iPad.

Swiping up and down

Swipe up and down with one finger to move up or down web pages, photos, maps or documents. The content moves in the opposite direction of the swipe, i.e. if you swipe up, the page will move down and vice versa.

The faster you swipe on the screen, the faster the screen moves up or down.

29

Tapping and zooming

Double-tap with one finger to zoom in on a web page, photo, map or document. Double-tap with two fingers to return to the original view.

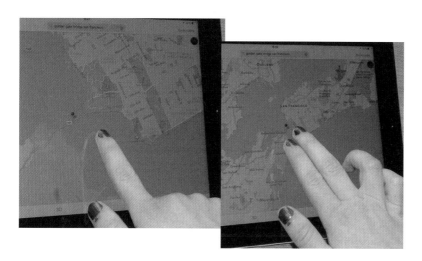

...cont'd

Pinching and swiping

Swipe outwards with thumb and forefinger to zoom in on a web page, photo, map or document.

Swiping outwards with thumb and forefinger enables you to zoom in on an item to a greater degree than double-tapping with one finger.

30

Pinch together with thumb and forefinger to zoom back out on a web page, photo, map or document.

More gestures

- Swipe left or right with four or five fingers to move between open apps

- Drag with two or three fingers to move a web page, photo, map or document

- Press and swipe down on any free area on the screen to access the Spotlight Search box

- Swipe left or right with one finger to move between full-size photos in the Photos app

- Tap once on a photo thumbnail with one finger to enlarge it to full screen within the Photos app

- Drag up from the bottom of the screen to access the Control Center

- Drag down at the top-middle of the iPad to view current notifications in the Notification Center

Hot tip

The Multitasking Gestures involving four or five fingers can be turned On or Off in the **General** section of the **Settings** app.

Finding Things with Siri

Siri is the iPad voice assistant that provides answers to a variety of questions by looking at your iPad and also web services. You can ask Siri questions relating to the apps on your iPad and also general questions, such as weather conditions around the world, or sports results. Initially, Siri can be set up within the **Settings** app:

32

1 In the **General** section, tap once on the **Siri** link

2 Drag the **Siri** button to On to activate the Siri functionality. Tap once on the links to select a language, set voice feedback and allow access to your details

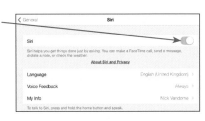

Questioning Siri

Once you have set up Siri, you can start putting it to work with your queries. To do this:

1 Hold down the **Home** button until the Siri window appears

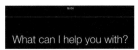

2 To find something from your iPad apps, ask a question such as, **Show me my reminders**

3 Tap once on the microphone button to ask another question of Siri

...cont'd

Siri can also find information from across the Web and related web services:

1 Siri can provide sports results, for certain sports in certain countries, such as in response to the question, **How did the Red Sox get on in their last match?**

2 Weather reports are another of Siri's strong points and can even add in a bit of editorial comment in response to the question, **What is the weather like in Valletta?**

3 However, even Siri's knowledge is limited and if there is a subject it does not recognize it will own up and offer to search the Web instead

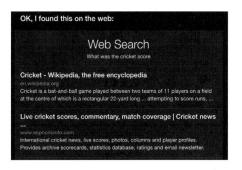

Siri can adapt to a number of different questioning styles, such as **Tell me about...**, **What is...**, **How can I get...**, and **How do I...**. The answers may be the same for each different style, although Siri may amend its comments, in the same way as people having a real conversation.

Searching with Spotlight

Siri can be used to search for items on your iPad and you can also use the built-in search engine, Spotlight. This can search over numerous items on your iPad and these can be selected within Settings:

Spotlight settings
Within the Settings app you can select which items the Spotlight search operates over. To do this:

Don't forget

To return to the Home screen from the Search page, tap once anywhere on the screen.

Hot tip

Enter the name of an app into the Spotlight search box and tap on the result to launch the app from here.

1 Tap once on the **Settings** app

2 Tap once on **General** tab

3 Tap once on the **Spotlight Search** link

Spotlight Search

4 Tap once on an item to exclude it from the Spotlight search. Items with a tick will be included

Accessing Spotlight
The Spotlight search box can be accessed from any screen by pressing and swiping downwards on any free area of the Home screen. This also activates the keyboard.

Hot tip

If you hide the keyboard when on the Search page, the Dock items become visible and can be selected. For details on hiding the keyboard, see Chapter Three.

Living in the iCloud

iCloud is the Apple online service that performs a number of valuable functions:

- It makes your content available across multiple devices. The content is stored in the iCloud and then pushed out to other iCloud-enabled devices, including the iPhone, iPod Touch and other Mac or Windows computers.

- It enables online access to your content via the iCloud website. This includes your iCloud email, contacts, calendar and reminders.

- It backs up the content on your iPad.

Once you have registered for and set up iCloud, it works automatically so you do not have to worry about anything. You can activate iCloud when you first set up your iPad, or:

It is free to register and set up a standard iCloud account.

To access your iCloud account through the website, access **www.icloud.com** and enter your Apple ID details (see page 79).

1 Tap once on the **Settings** app

2 Tap once on the **iCloud** tab

3 Tap once on the **Account** link

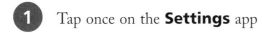

4 Enter your Apple ID and password to set up iCloud on your iPad

The **Account** window also has details of your iCloud email account.

...cont'd

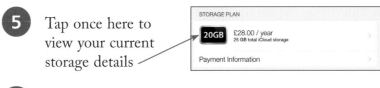

5 Tap once here to view your current storage details

6 Upgrade options are displayed. Tap once on this button and then select the free 5GB storage option

By default, you get 5GB of free storage space with an iCloud account. Make sure you select the **Downgrade Options** and choose the **Free Plan** to ensure you do not automatically get put onto a paid-for storage Plan. (Correct at the time of printing.)

iCloud settings

Once you have set up your iCloud account you can then apply settings for how it works. Once you have done this you will not have to worry about it again:

1 Access the **iCloud** section in the Settings app, as above

2 Drag these buttons to On for each item that you wish to be included in iCloud. Each item is then saved and stored in the iCloud and made available to your other iCloud-enabled devices

The Apple iWork apps, Pages, Keynote and Numbers, have their content saved into the **iCloud** under **Documents & Data**.

3 Tap once on the **Photos** and **Documents & Data** links to access the buttons for turning these On, including using the **Photo Stream** option for sharing your photos with other people

iCloud Storage & Backup

It is possible to view how the storage on your iCloud account is being used and also specify how your content is backed up to iCloud. To do this:

1 Access the iCloud section in the Settings app, as above, and tap once on **Storage & Backup**

Tap once on the **Back Up Now** button at Step 4 to perform a manual backup of your iPad content.

2 Tap once on the **Manage Storage** link to view how your iCloud storage is being used

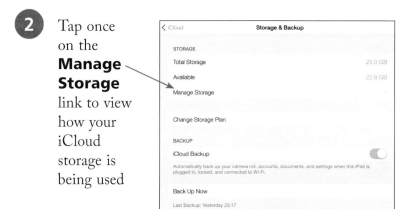

3 Tap once on an app to view the individual documents within it that are being stored

Another useful iCloud function is the iCloud Keychain **(Settings > iCloud > Keychain)**. If this is enabled, it can keep all of your passwords and credit card information up-to-date across multiple devices and remember them when you use them on websites. The information is encrypted and controlled through your Apple ID.

4 Drag this button to On to enable automatic backups

Updating Software

The operating system that powers the iPad is known as iOS. This is a mobile computing operating system and it is also used on the iPhone and the iPod Touch. The latest version is iOS 7. Periodically, there are updates to the iOS to fix bugs and add new features. These can be downloaded to your iPad once they are released:

If your iOS software is up-to-date there is a message to this effect in the **Software Update** window.

1 Tap once on the **Settings** app

2 Tap once on the **General** tab

3 Tap once on the **Software Update** link

4 If there is an update available it will be displayed here, with details of what is contained within it

It is always worth updating the iOS to keep up-to-date with fixes. Also, app developers update their products to use the latest iOS features.

5 Tap once here to start the downloading process. The iOS update will then be done automatically

Using the Lock Screen

To save power it is possible to set your iPad screen to auto-lock. This is the equivalent of the sleep option on a traditional computer. To do this:

1 Tap once on the **Settings** app

2 Tap once on the **General** tab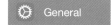

3 Tap once on the **Auto-Lock** link

Auto-Lock	Never >

4 Tap once on the time of non-use after which you wish the screen to be locked

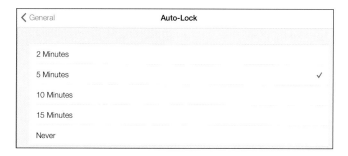

5 Once the screen is locked, swipe here to the right to unlock the screen

The screen can also be locked by clicking once on the On/Off button at the top of the iPad.

Auto-locking the screen does not prevent other people from accessing your iPad. If you want to prevent anyone else having access, it can be locked with a passcode. See Chapter 12 for details.

iPad Smart Cover

To prevent the iPad screen getting scratched, a cover (known as a Smart Cover) can be used as protection. This can also be used as a stand to support the iPad for viewing content or typing with the keyboard.

There are settings for the iPad cover in the Settings app. This can enable it to lock or unlock the iPad:

Don't forget

Smart Covers come in a variety of colors and there are also leather ones available.

1 Tap once on the **Settings** app

2 Tap once on the **General** tab

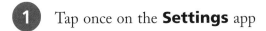

3 Under **Lock/ Unlock** drag the

button to On to enable the cover to lock or unlock the iPad when it is placed in position or removed

Attaching the cover

The iPad cover attaches with a hinge along the left-hand side of the iPad. Attach it by placing the hinge on the side of the iPad until it clicks magnetically into place.

Using the cover as a stand

The iPad cover is separated into four foldable panels. These can be folded into a triangular shape to create a stand for the iPad.

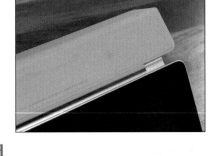

Don't forget

Use the stand at the top of the iPad when using the keyboard for input options. Use it at the bottom of the iPad when viewing content such as videos or photos.

Accessibility Issues

The iPad tries to cater to as wide a range of users as possible, including those who have difficulty with vision, hearing or physical and motor issues. There are a number of settings that can help with these areas. To access the range of accessibility settings:

1 Tap once on the **Settings** app

2 Tap once on the **General** tab

3 Tap once on the **Accessibility** link

4 The settings for **Vision**, **Hearing**, **Learning** and **Physical & Motor** are displayed here

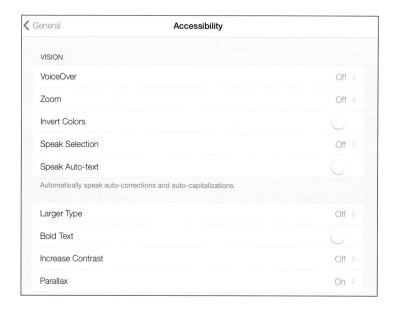

...cont'd

Vision settings

These can help anyone with impaired vision and there are options to hear items on the screen and also for making text easier to read:

Don't forget

When VoiceOver is On, tap once on an item to select it and have it spoken; double-tap to activate the item.

1 Tap once on the **VoiceOver** link

VoiceOver	Off >

2 Drag this button to On to activate the VoiceOver function. This then enables items to be spoken when you tap on them

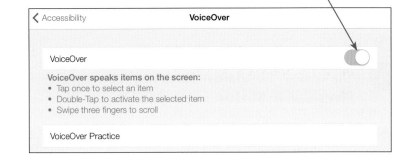

< Accessibility   **VoiceOver**

VoiceOver

VoiceOver speaks items on the screen:
- Tap once to select an item
- Double-Tap to activate the selected item
- Swipe three fingers to scroll

VoiceOver Practice

Hot tip

There is a wide range of options for the way VoiceOver can be used. For full details see the Apple website at **www.apple.com/ accessibility/ios/**

3 Select options for VoiceOver as required

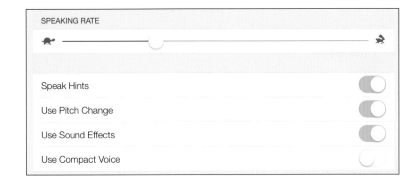

SPEAKING RATE

Speak Hints

Use Pitch Change

Use Sound Effects

Use Compact Voice

4 Tap once on the **Accessibility** button to return to the main options

5 Tap once on these buttons to access options for zooming the screen, increasing text size, inverting the text color on the screen and speaking text options

6 Tap once on the **Accessibility** button to return to the main options after each selection

Hearing settings

These can be used to change the iPad speaker from stereo to mono. To do this:

1 Drag this button to On to enable **Mono Audio**

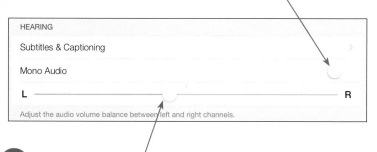

2 Drag this button to specify whether sound comes out of the left or the right side of the speaker

If you turn on the **Zoom** function you can magnify the whole screen by double-tapping twice. To move around the screen, drag with three fingers. To change the amount of zoom, double-tap with three fingers and drag up or down on the screen.

43

The **Speak Auto-text** function can be turned on so that auto-corrections and auto-capitalizations are automatically spoken.

...cont'd

AssistiveTouch

This can be used by anyone who has difficulty navigating around the iPad with the screen or buttons. It can be used with an external device such as a joystick, or it can be used on its own. To use AssistiveTouch:

1 Tap once on the **AssistiveTouch** link

PHYSICAL & MOTOR	
Switch Control	Off >
AssistiveTouch	Off >

Don't forget

The **AssistiveTouch** options make it easier for anyone with difficulties clicking the Home button, or using Multitasking Gestures.

2 Drag this button to On to activate the **AssistiveTouch** function

‹ Accessibility	**AssistiveTouch**	Edit
AssistiveTouch		◯

3 The AssistiveTouch icon appears on the screen and can be dragged around

4 Tap once on the AssistiveTouch icon to view its options

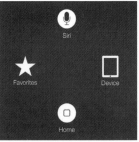

5 Tap once on the **Home** icon to return to the Home screen

6 Tap once on the **Favorites** icon to access options for using custom gestures

7 To create a custom gesture, tap once on this link under the AssitiveTouch section

8 Drag on the screen with the required gesture (e.g. swiping with four fingers to move between open apps)

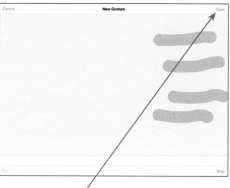

9 Tap once on the **Save** button

10 Give the gesture a name and tap once on the **Save** button

11 The gesture is added under the Favorites section

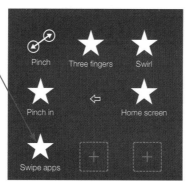

12 Tap once on a gesture to select it. The corresponding number of blue circles appear. Tap on one to activate the gesture

Don't forget

The **Gestures** section can be used to perform Multitasking Gestures, without having to physically use the full number of fingers on the screen.

45

Hot tip

The **Favorites** section can also be used to create custom gestures. To do this, tap once on one of the empty boxes and then record the gesture in the **New Gesture** window. Once it is saved it becomes available in the Favorites section.

...cont'd

13 Tap once on the **Device** icon

14 Tap once to activate the required function, including changing the screen rotation and adjusting the volume

Guided Access

The Guided Access option allows for certain functionality within an app to be disabled so that individual tasks can be focused on without any other distractions. To use this:

1 Under the Learning heading tap once on the **Guided Access** link

> LEARNING
>
> Guided Access   Off >

2 Drag this button to On to activate the Guided Access functionality

3 Open an app and triple-click on the **Home** button to activate Guided Access within the app

4 Circle an area on the screen to disable it (this can be any functionality within the app). Tap on the **Start** button to activate Guided Access for that app. The circled area will not function within the app

3 The iPad Keyboard

The iPad has a virtual keyboard rather than a traditional one. This chapter shows how to use it and also edit text and add shortcuts.

48 It's Virtually a Keyboard

50 Keyboard Settings

52 Entering Text

53 Editing Text

55 Moving the Keyboard

57 Keyboard Shortcuts

60 Voice Typing

It's Virtually a Keyboard

The keyboard on the iPad is a virtual one, i.e. it appears on the touch screen whenever text or numbered input is required for an app. This can be for a variety of reasons:

- Entering text with a word processing app, email or an organizing app such as Notes

- Entering a web address in a web browser such as the Safari app

- Entering information into a form

- Entering a password

Viewing the keyboard

When you attempt one of the items above, the keyboard appears so that you can enter any text or numbers:

Around the keyboard

To access the various keyboard controls:

Don't forget

In addition to the iPad virtual keyboard, it is also possible to use a traditional computer keyboard with the iPad. This can be particularly useful if you are using the iPad for a lot of typing. The keyboard is an Apple Wireless Keyboard which connects via Bluetooth. This can be turned on in the Settings app, under the Bluetooth tab.

Don't forget

To return from Caps Lock, tap once on the Caps button.

48

1 Tap once on this button to create a **Cap** (capital) text letter

2 Double-tap on this button to create **Caps Lock**

3 Tap once on this button to back delete an item

4 Tap once on this button to access the **Numbers** keyboard option

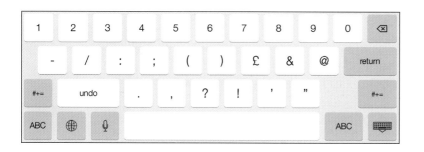

If you are entering a password, or details into a form, the keyboard will have a **Go** or **Send** button that can be used to activate the information that has been entered.

5 From the Numbers keyboard, tap once on this button to access the **Symbols** keyboard

6 Tap once on this button on either of the two keyboards above to return to the standard QWERTY option

The button in Step 7 can also be used to undock and move the keyboard. For details see pages 55-56.

7 Tap once on this button to hide the keyboard (this can be done from any of the keyboard options). If the keyboard is hidden, tap once on one of the input options, e.g. entering text, to show it again

Keyboard Settings

Settings for the keyboard can be determined in the General section of the Settings app. To do this:

1 Tap once on the **Settings** app

2 Tap once on the **General** tab

3 Tap once on the **Keyboard** link

Keyboard	>

4 Drag this slider to On to enable **Auto-Capitalization**, i.e. letters will automatically be capitalized at the beginning of a sentence

5 Drag this slider to On to enable **Auto-Correction**, i.e. suggestions for words will appear as you type, particularly if you have mis-typed a word

Auto-Correction

6 Drag this slider to On to check spelling as you type

Hot tip

The Auto-Correction function works as you type a word, so it may change a number of times, depending on the length of the word you are typing.

7 Drag this slider to On to enable the **Caps Lock** function to be performed

8 Drag this slider to On to enable the **Shortcut** functionality

Don't forget

For more information about keyboard shortcuts, see pages 57-59.

9 Drag this slider to On to enable the keyboard to be split and moved. Tap once on the Keyboards link to access options for adding different international keyboards

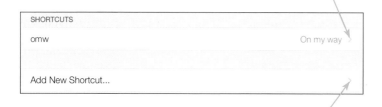

10 Tap once on this link to view existing text shortcuts and also to create new ones

SHORTCUTS

omw   On my way

Add New Shortcut...

11 Tap once on this link to create new shortcuts

Entering Text

Once you have applied the keyboard settings that you require you can start entering text. To do this:

1 Tap once on the screen to activate the keyboard. Start typing with the keyboard. The text will appear at the point where you tapped on the screen

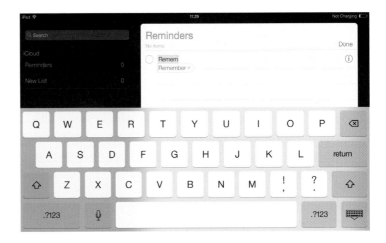

2 As you type, Auto-Correction comes up with suggestions. Tap once on the spacebar to accept the suggestion, or tap once on the cross next to it to reject it

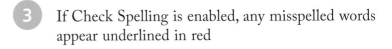

3 If Check Spelling is enabled, any misspelled words appear underlined in red

Remember to go to the supermrket

4 Tap once on this button to hide the keyboard

Don't forget

If you keep typing as normal, the Auto-Correction suggestion will disappear when you finish the word.

Editing Text

Once text has been entered it can be selected, copied, cut and pasted. Depending on the app being used, the text can also be formatted, such as with a word processing app.

Selecting text

To select text and perform tasks on it:

1 To change the insertion point, tap and hold until the magnifying glass appears

2 Drag the magnifying glass to move the insertion point

3 Tap once at the insertion point to access the selection buttons

4 Double-tap on a word to select it. Tap once on **Cut** or **Copy** as required

5 Drag the selection handles to expand or contract the selection

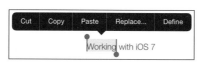

6 If text has been copied, tap and hold at a new point on the page and tap once on **Paste**

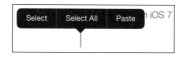

Hot tip

Once the selection buttons have been accessed, tap once on **Select** to select the previous word, or **Select All** to select all of the text.

...cont'd

Formatting text

Once text has been added to a document it can be formatted in a number of ways (depending on the app). To do this:

1 Select text in a document as shown on the previous page. Instead of copying it, it can be formatted with buttons within the app (this is for the Pages app)

2 Tap once on these buttons to, from left to right, change the font, decrease the font size, set a specific font size and increase the font size

3 Tap once on these buttons to, from left to right, create bold, italic or underlined text or set the text alignment

Don't forget

Some apps that allow text entry have formatting options, while others do not and text is just entered in a standard format.

Moving the Keyboard

By default, the keyboard appears as a single unit along the bottom of the screen. However, it is possible to split the keyboard so that it appears on separate sides of the screen. It is also possible to undock the keyboard and move it around the screen.

Undocking the keyboard

To undock the keyboard from its position at the bottom of the screen:

1 Press and hold on this button on the keyboard

2 Tap once on the **Undock** button

3 The keyboard is undocked from the bottom of the screen

To redock the keyboard, tap and hold on the button in Step 1 and tap once on the **Dock** button.

4 Tap and hold here at the side of the button to move the keyboard

5 The keyboard can then be moved to different positions around the screen

...cont'd

Splitting the keyboard

The keyboard can also be split into two and used on either side of the screen. To do this:

Beware

When the keyboard is split, both sides can be a bit small and it is a bit more fiddly than using the full-size keyboard.

Hot tip

The keyboard can also be split by swiping outwards on either side with one finger.

1 Press and hold on this button on the keyboard

2 Tap once on the **Split** button

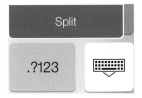

3 The keyboard is split to the left and the right sides of the screen

4 Press and hold here to move the split keyboard

5 Press and hold on the button above and tap once on the **Dock and Merge** button to return the keyboard to its default position at the bottom of the screen

Keyboard Shortcuts

There are two types of shortcuts that can be used on the iPad keyboard:

- Shortcuts on the keys on the keyboard

- Shortcuts created with text abbreviations

Shortcuts with keys

The shortcuts that can be created with the keys on the keyboard are:

1 Double-tap on the spacebar to add a full stop/period and a space at the end of a sentence

2 Swipe up once on the comma (or press and hold) to insert an apostrophe

3 Swipe up once on the full stop/period to insert quotation marks

4 Press and hold on appropriate letters to access accented versions for different languages

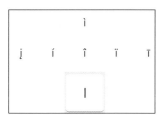

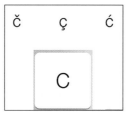

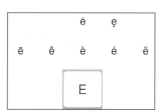

Hot tip

The shortcut in Step 1 can be disabled by switching off the Shortcut option within the **Settings > General > Keyboard** section.

...cont'd

Text abbreviations

To create shortcuts with text abbreviations:

1 Tap once on the **Settings** app

2 Tap once on the **General** tab

3 Tap once on the **Keyboard** link

> Keyboard   >

Beware

An abbreviation for a shortcut has to have a minimum of two characters.

4 Tap once on the **Add New Shortcut...** link

SHORTCUTS	
omw	On my way >
Add New Shortcut...	>

5 Enter the phrase you want to be made into a shortcut

Phrase	My name is Nick

6 Enter the abbreviation you want to use as the shortcut for the phrase

Shortcut	mnn

7 Tap once on the **Save** button

Save

8 The shortcut is displayed here

Don't forget

The abbreviation does not have to have the equivalent number of letters as words in the phrase. A 10-word phrase could have a two-letter abbreviation.

SHORTCUTS	
mnn	My name is Nick >

Using shortcuts

Once you have created shortcuts you can then use them with the iPad keyboard. To do this:

① Enter the abbreviation. As you type, the phrase appears underneath the abbreviation

② Tap once on the spacebar to add the phrase, or tap once on the cross to reject it

Deleting shortcuts

Shortcuts can be deleted, if you do not want to use them anymore. To do this:

The shortcut abbreviation is not case sensitive, i.e. you can enter it in upper or lower case and the same phrase will appear from the shortcut item.

① In the Keyboard section of the General Settings, tap once on the **Edit** button

Edit

② Tap once on the red circle next to the shortcut you want to delete

③ Tap once on the **Delete** button to remove the shortcut

Abbreviation shortcuts work even if the Auto-Correction function has been disabled.

④ Tap once on the **Done** button

Done

Voice Typing

On the keyboard there is also a voice typing option, which enables you to enter text by speaking into a microphone, rather than typing on the keyboard. This is On by default.

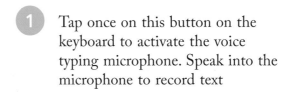

Using voice typing

Voice typing can be used with any app with a text input function. To do this:

Beware

Voice typing is not an exact science and you may find that some strange examples appear. The best results are created if you speak as clearly as possible and reasonably slowly.

1 Tap once on this button on the keyboard to activate the voice typing microphone. Speak into the microphone to record text

2 As the voice typing function is processing the recording this screen appears

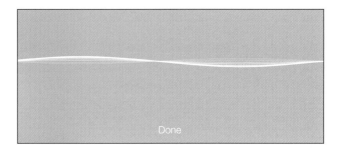

Done

Don't forget

There are other voice typing apps available from the App Store. Two to try are Dragon Dictation and Voice Dictation.

3 Tap once on the **Done** button to finish recording

4 Once the recording has been processed the text appears in the app

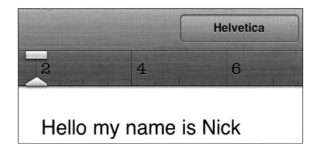

Helvetica

Hello my name is Nick

4 Knowing your Apps

Apps are the parts that keep the iPad engine running. This chapter details the built-in ones and also shows how to access and use apps from the App Store.

62 What is an App?

63 Built-in Apps

66 About the App Store

68 Finding Apps

72 Downloading Apps

73 Updating Apps

74 Organizing Apps

76 Deleting Apps

You need an active Internet connection to download apps from the App Store.

Within a number of apps there is a **Share** button that can be used to share items through a variety of methods, including email, Facebook and Twitter. For the iPad 4 and later and the iPad Mini the Share button can also be used to share items using the AirDrop function over short distances with other compatible devices. To access these options, tap once on this button, where available.

What is an App?

An app is just a more modern name for a computer program. Initially, it was used in relation to mobile devices, such as the iPhone and the iPad, but it is now becoming more widely used with desktop and laptop computers, for both Mac and Windows operating systems.

On the iPad there are two types of apps:

- **Built-in apps.** These are the apps that come pre-installed on the iPad.

- **App Store apps.** These are apps that can be downloaded from the online App Store. There is a huge range of apps available there, covering a variety of different categories. Some are free while others have to be paid for. The apps in the App Store are updated and added to on a daily basis so there are always new ones to explore.

There are also two important points about apps (both built-in and those from the App Store) to remember:

- Apart from some of the built-in apps, the majority of apps do not interact with each other. This means that there is less chance of viruses being transmitted from app to app on your iPad and they can operate without a reliance on other apps.

- Content created by apps is saved within the app itself, rather than within a file structure on your iPad, e.g. if you create a note in the Notes app, it is saved there, if you take a photo, it is saved in the Photos app. Content is usually also saved automatically when it is created, or edited, so you do not have to worry about saving it as you work on it.

Built-in Apps

The built-in iPad apps are the ones that appear on the Home screen when you turn on the iPad:

The iPad **Settings** app is another of the built-in apps and this is looked at in detail in Chapter Two.

- **App Store.** This can be used to access the App Store, from where additional apps can then be downloaded.

- **Calendar.** An app for storing appointments, important dates and other calendar information. It can be synced with iCloud.

- **Camera.** This gives direct access to the front-facing and rear-facing iPad cameras.

- **Clock.** This displays the current time and can be used to view the time in different countries and also as an alarm clock and a stopwatch.

- **Contacts.** An address book app. Once contacts are added here they can then also be accessed from other apps, such as Mail.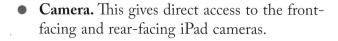

Some of the built-in apps, such as Mail and Contacts, interact with each other. However, since these are designed by Apple there is almost no chance of them containing viruses.

...cont'd

Beware

You need an Apple ID to obtain iBooks. They are downloaded in a matter of seconds and you cannot change your mind once you have entered your Apple ID details. For full details about obtaining an Apple ID, see Chapter Five.

- **FaceTime.** This is an app that uses the built-in FaceTime camera on the iPad to hold video chats with other iPad users, or those with an iPhone, iPod Touch or a Mac computer.

- **Game Center.** For those who like gaming, this is an app for playing a variety of games, either individually or with friends.

- **iBooks.** This is an app for downloading electronic books, which can then be read on the iPad. This can be done for plain text or illustrated iBooks. Although this is considered a built-in app, it has to first be downloaded from the App Store.

- **iTunes Store.** This app can be used to browse the iTunes store where music, TV shows, movies and more, can be downloaded to your iPad.

- **Mail.** This is the email app for sending and receiving email on your iPad.

- **Maps.** Use this app to view maps from around the world, find specific locations and get directions to destinations.

- **Messages.** This is the iPad messaging service, which can be used between iPads, iPhones, iPod Touches and Mac computers. It can be used with not only text but also photos and videos.

- **Music.** An app for playing music on your iPad and also viewing cover artwork. You can also use it to create your own playlists.

- **Newsstand.** Similar to iBooks, this app can be used to download and read newspapers and magazines.

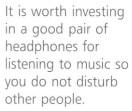

- **Notes.** If you need to jot down your thoughts or ideas, this app is perfect for just that.

- **Photo Booth.** A photography app that can be used to create distorted and special effects photos of people or objects.

- **Photos.** This is an app for viewing and editing photos and creating slideshows.

It is worth investing in a good pair of headphones for listening to music so you do not disturb other people.

- **Reminders.** Use this app for organization, when you want to create to-do lists and set reminders for events.

- **Safari.** The Apple web browser that has been developed for viewing the Web on your iPad.

- **Videos.** This is an app for viewing videos on your iPad and also streaming them to a larger HDTV monitor.

About the App Store

While the built-in apps that come with the iPad are flexible and versatile, it really comes into its own when you connect to the App Store. This is an online resource and there are thousands of apps there that can be downloaded and then used on your iPad, including categories from Lifestyle to Travel and Medical.

To use the App Store, you must first have an Apple ID. This can be obtained when you first connect to the App Store. Once you have an Apple ID you can start exploring the App Store:

Don't forget

For full details about obtaining an Apple ID, see Chapter Five.

66

1 Tap once on the **App Store** app on the Home screen

2 The latest available apps are displayed on the homepage of the App Store, including the Editor's Choice, featured in the top panel

3 Tap on these buttons to view the apps according to **Featured**, **Top Charts**, **Near Me**, **Purchased** and **Updates**

Viewing apps

To view apps in the App Store and read about their content and functionality:

1 Tap once on an app

2 General details about the app are displayed

3 Swipe left or right here to view additional information about the app and view details

4 Reviews and related apps are available from the relevant buttons, next to the **Details** button

Don't forget

If it is an upgraded version of an app, this page will include details of any fixes and improvements that have been made.

Finding Apps

Featured

Within the App Store, apps are separated into categories according to type. This enables you to find apps according to particular subjects. To do this:

1 Tap once on the **Featured** button on the toolbar at the bottom of the App Store

2 Scroll left and right to view different category headings

3 Scroll up the page to view additional categories and **Quick Links**

4 Use these buttons at the top of the window to refine the categories for looking for apps

Don't forget

Some apps will differ depending on the geographical location from where you are accessing the App Store.

Hot tip

Tap on the **More** button in Step 4 to view all of the categories within the App Store.

...cont'd

Top Charts
To find the top rated apps:

1 Tap once on the **Top Charts** button on the toolbar at the bottom of the App Store

2 The top overall paid for, free and top grossing apps are displayed

Do not limit yourself to just viewing the top apps. Although these are the most popular, there are also a lot of excellent apps within each category.

3 To find the top apps in different categories, tap once on this button

Categories

4 Tap once on a category

5 The top apps for that category are displayed

Depending on your location, there may not be any apps featured in the **Near Me** section.

...cont'd

Near Me

This is a feature which suggests appropriate apps according to your current geographic location. To use this:

1 Tap once on the **Near Me** button on the toolbar at the bottom of the App Store

2 Tap once on the **Show Popular Apps Near Me** link

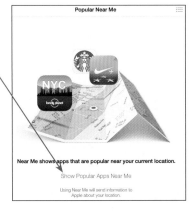

3 Tap once on the **OK** button to enable the App Store to use your location (**Location Services** have to be turned On)

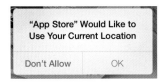

4 Recommendations will appear in the **Popular Near Me** window, based on your location

...cont'd

Searching for apps

Another way to find apps is with the App Store Search box, which is located at the top-right corner of the App Store window. To use this:

1 Tap once in the **Search** box to bring up the iPad virtual keyboard

For more information about using the iPad virtual keyboard see Chapter Three.

2 Enter a search keyword or phrase

3 Suggested apps appear as you are typing

4 Tap once on an app to view it

Downloading Apps

When you identify an app that you would like to use, it can be downloaded to your iPad. To do this:

Don't forget

Apps usually download in a few minutes, or less, depending on the speed of your Wi-Fi connection.

Beware

Some apps have 'in-app purchases'. This is additional content that has to be paid for when it is downloaded.

1 Find the app you want to download and tap once on the button next to the app (this will say Free or will have a price)

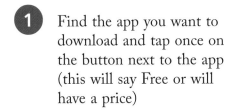

2 The button changes to show **Install**. Tap on this once

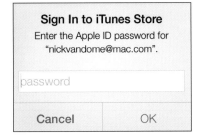
Sign In to iTunes Store
Enter the Apple ID password for "nickvandome@mac.com".

password

Cancel   OK

3 Enter your Apple ID details and tap once on the **OK** button

4 The app will begin to download on your iPad

NATIONAL GEOGRAPHIC
CITIES
Loading...

5 Once the app is downloaded tap once on it to open and use it

fotopedia
Heritage

Hill Climb

in easy steps
In Easy Steps

NATIONAL GEOGRAPHIC
CITIES
City Guides

Updating Apps

The world of apps is a dynamic and fast-moving one and new apps are being created and added to the App Store on a daily basis. Existing apps are also being updated, to improve their performance and functionality. Once you have installed an app from the App Store it is possible to obtain updates, at no extra cost (if the app was paid for). To do this:

1 When an update is available it is denoted by a red icon on the App Store app, showing how many updates are available

2 Tap once on the **App Store** app

3 In the App Store, tap once on the **Updates** button

4 The available updates are displayed

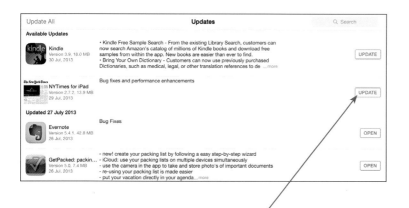

5 Tap once on the button next to an app to update it

6 Tap once on the **Update All** button to update all of the required apps

You should keep your apps as up-to-date as possible to take advantage of software fixes and any updates to the iPad operating system (iOS).

It is possible to set updates to apps to be downloaded automatically: **Settings > iTunes & App Stores > Automatic Downloads**. Drag the button to On for the required items.

Organizing Apps

When you start downloading apps you will probably soon find that you have dozens, if not hundreds, of them. You can move between screens to view all of your apps by swiping left or right with one finger.

Hot tip

To move an app between screens, tap and hold on it until it starts to jiggle and a cross appears in the corner. Then drag it to the side of the screen. If there is space on the next screen the app will be moved there.

As more apps are added it can become hard to find the apps you want, particularly if you have to swipe between several screens. However, it is possible to organize apps into individual folders to make using them more manageable. To do this:

1 Press on an app until it starts to jiggle and a white cross appears at the top-left corner

2 Drag the app over another one

3 A folder is created, containing the two apps

4 The folder is given a default name, usually based on the category of the apps

5 Tap on the folder name and type a new name if required

6 Click the **Home** button once to finish creating the folder

7 Click the **Home** button again to return to the Home screen (this is done whenever you want to return to the Home screen from an apps folder)

8 The folder is added on the Home screen. Tap once on this to access the items within it

Only top-level folders can be created, i.e. sub-folders cannot be created. Also, one folder cannot be placed within another.

If you want to rename an apps folder after it has been created, tap and hold on it until it starts to jiggle. Then tap on it once and edit the folder name as in Step 5.

75

Deleting Apps

If you decide that you do not want certain apps anymore, they can be deleted from your iPad. However, they remain in the iCloud so that you can reinstall them if you change your mind. This also means that if you delete an app by mistake you can get it back from the App Store without having to pay for it again. To do this:

If you delete an app it will also delete any data that has been compiled with that app, even if you reinstall it from the App Store.

1 Press on an app until it starts to jiggle and a white cross appears at the top-left corner

2 Tap once on the white cross to delete the app. In the Delete dialog box, tap once on the **Delete** button

Delete "Pages"
Deleting "Pages" will also delete all of its data from this iPad. Any documents & data stored in iCloud will not be deleted and can be managed in Settings.

Delete   Cancel

3 Tap once on the **App Store** app

App Store

You cannot delete any of the built-in iPad apps, even by mistake.

4 Tap once on the **Purchased** button

Purchased

5 Apps that have been deleted have this iCloud icon next to them

Pages
Apple
Version 2.0.1

6 Tap once on the **iCloud** button to reinstall an app

5 Keeping in Touch

This chapter shows how to use your iPad to keep ahead in the fast- moving world of online communications, using email, social networking, video calls, messaging and Skype.

78 Getting Online

79 Obtaining an Apple ID

80 Setting up an Email Account

82 Emailing

85 Adding Social Networking

86 Having a Video Chat

88 Messaging

90 Phoning with Skype

92 Communication Apps

Getting Online

iPads can be used for a variety of different communications, but they all require online access. This is done via Wi-Fi and you will need to have an Internet Service Provider and a Wi-Fi router to connect to the Internet. Once this is in place you will be able to connect to a Wi-Fi network:

Don't forget

If you have the 4G version of the iPad you can obtain Internet access this way, but this has to be done through a provider of this service, as with a cell/mobile phone.

Don't forget

If you are connecting to your home Wi-Fi network the iPad should connect automatically each time, after it has been set up. If you are connecting in a public Wi-Fi area you will be asked which network you would like to join.

1 Tap once on the **Settings** app

2 Tap once on the **Wi-Fi** tab

| 🛜 Wi-Fi | Not Connected |

3 Ensure the **Wi-Fi** button is in the On position

| Wi-Fi | 🔘 |

4 Available networks are shown here. Tap once on one to select it

CHOOSE A NETWORK...
NETGEAR	🔒 🛜 ⓘ
virginmedia6249958	🔒 🛜 ⓘ
Diagnostic Mode	›

5 Enter a password for your Wi-Fi router

Enter the password for "NETGEAR"
Cancel   **Enter Password**   Join
Password   ••••••••

6 Tap once on the **Join** button   Join

7 Once a network has been joined, a tick appears next to it. This now provides access to the Internet

| Wi-Fi | 🔘 |
| ✓ NETGEAR | 🔒 🛜 ⓘ |

Obtaining an Apple ID

An Apple ID is a registered email address and password with Apple that enables you to log in and use a variety of online Apple services. These include:

- App Store
- iTunes Store
- iCloud
- iMessage
- FaceTime
- Game Center
- iBooks

It is free to register for an Apple ID and this can be done when you access one of the apps or services which requires this, or you can do it on the Apple website at My Apple ID (**https://appleid.apple.com**):

Hot tip

If you are using an Apple ID to buy items, such as from iTunes or the App Store, you will need to provide a valid method of payment.

1. Tap once on the **Create an Apple ID** button

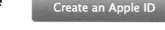

2. Enter your email address and a password

Create an Apple ID.

Choose an Apple ID and password.
Enter your primary email address as your Apple ID. This will be used as the contact email address for your account. Please note that this email address must be verified before you can use certain Apple services.

Apple ID   @mac.com

Password   ••••••••

Confirm Password   ••••••••

Create a security question.
Select a security question or create one of your own. This question will help us verify your identity should you forget your password.

3. Enter additional details and enter the security code and tap once on the **Create Apple ID** button

Please type the characters you see in the image below.

QCTGR

↻ Try a different image
◀⦚ Vision Impaired

QCTGR
Letters are not case sensitive.

☑ I have read and agree to the Apple Terms of Service and Apple Customer Privacy Policy.

Cancel   Create Apple ID

Don't forget

My Apple ID is where you can access your Apple ID details and edit them, if required.

Setting up an Email Account

Email accounts

Email settings can be specified within the Settings app. Different email accounts can also be added there.

1 Tap once on the **Settings** app

2 Tap once on the **Mail, Contacts, Calendars** link

3 Tap once on the **Add Account** link to add a new account

ACCOUNTS

iCloud
Mail, Contacts, Calendars, Safari, Reminders, Notes, Photos, Find My iPad and 2 more... >

Add Account >

4 Tap once on the type of email account you want to add

< Mail, Contacts... **Add Account**

iCloud
Exchange
Gmail
YAHOO!

5 Enter the details for the account. Tap once on the **Next** button

Cancel **Gmail** Next

Name Nick Vandome

Email nickvandome@googlemail.com

Password ••••••••

Description nickvandome@googlemail.com

6 Drag these buttons On or Off to specify which functions are to be available for the required account

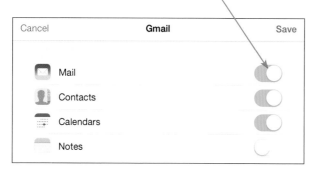

7 Each new account is added under the **Accounts** heading of the Mail, Contacts, Calendars section

Email settings

Email settings can be specified within the Settings app. Different email accounts can also be added there.

1 Under the Mail section there are several options for how Mail operates and looks. These include the number of messages being displayed, previewing emails and font size

Don't forget

If you set up more than one email account, messages from all of them can be downloaded and displayed by **Mail**.

Hot tip

The Threads option can be turned On to show connected email conversations within your Inbox. If there is a thread of emails this is indicated by this symbol. Tap on it once to view the thread.

Emailing

Email on the iPad is created, sent and received using the Mail app. This provides a range of functionality for managing email, including adding mailboxes and viewing email conversation threads.

Accessing Mail

To access Mail and start sending and receiving emails:

Hot tip

To quickly delete an email from your Inbox, swipe on it from right to left and tap once on the **Delete** button.

Don't forget

If the **Fetch New Data** option in the **Mail, Contacts, Calendar** Setting is set to **Push**, new emails will be downloaded automatically from your mail server. To check manually for new downloads, swipe down from the top of the mailbox pane.

1 Tap once on the **Mail** app (the red icon in the corner displays the number of unread emails in your Inbox)

2 Tap once on a message to display it in the main panel

3 Use these buttons to, from left to right, flag a message, move a message, delete a message, respond to a message and create a new message

4 Tap once on this button to reply to a message, forward it to a new recipient, save an image in a message or print it

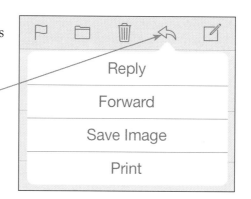

Creating email

To create and send an email:

1 Tap once on this button to create a new message

2 Enter a recipient name in the To box, or tap on one of the suggestions to select it

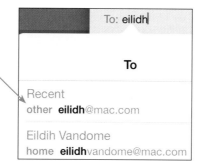

3 Enter a subject

Subject: **Lunch tomorrow?**

4 Enter the body text

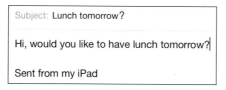

5 Tap once on the **Send** button to send the email to the recipient

...cont'd

Mailboxes

Different categories of email messages can be managed via Mailboxes. For instance, you may want to keep your social emails separately from ones that apply to financial activities.

Hot tip

Messages can be edited within individual mailboxes. To do this, select a mailbox and tap once on the **Edit** button. The message can then be edited with the **Delete**, **Move** or **Mark** options at the bottom of the window.

Don't forget

One mailbox that can be included is for VIPs, i.e. your most important contacts. To add these from an email, tap and hold on the person's name in an email you receive from them and tap once on the **Add to VIP** button. Under **Mailboxes**, tap once on **VIP** to view emails from all of your VIPs.

1   From your Inbox, tap once on the **iCloud** button

2   The current mailboxes are displayed. Tap once on the **Edit** button

3   Tap once on the **New Mailbox** button at the bottom of the Mailboxes panel

New Mailbox

4   Enter a name for the new mailbox. Tap once on the **Save** button

5   Tap once on the **Done** button

Done

6   To delete a mailbox, tap on it, then tap once on the **Delete Mailbox** button

Adding Social Networking

Using social networking sites such as Facebook, Twitter and Flickr to keep in touch with families and friends has now become common across all generations. On the iPad with iOS 7 it is possible to link to these accounts so that you can share content to them from your iPad and also view updates through the Notification Center and Safari. To do this:

1 Tap once on the **Settings** app

2 Select the required social networking option in the left-hand panel

Updates from Twitter can appear in your **Shared Links** section from within the web browser, Safari. See Chapter Six, page 101 for details.

3 Tap on the **Install** button to download the relevant app

4 Enter your login details for your account, or tap on the **Create New Account** button

Updates can be set to appear in your **Notification Center**. Open **Settings** and tap once on the **Notification Center** tab. Under the **Include** heading, tap once on the social networking site and select options for how you would like the notifications to appear.

5 Once you have set up your account, tap on the **Share** button, where it is available, to share content with your social networking sites

Having a Video Chat

Video chatting is a very personal and interactive way to keep in touch with family and friends around the world. The FaceTime app provides this facility with other iOS 5, iOS 6 and iOS 7 users on the iPad, iPhone and iPod Touch, or a Mac computer with FaceTime. To use FaceTime for video chatting:

1 Tap once on the **FaceTime** app

2 Sign in using your Apple ID to create your FaceTime account

To make video calls with FaceTime you need an active Internet connection.

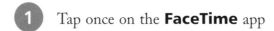

3 Tap once on the **Contacts** button

4 Tap once on a contact to access their details for making a FaceTime call

5 Tap once on their phone number or email address to make a FaceTime call. The recipient must have FaceTime on their iPad, iPhone, iPod Touch or Mac computer

6 Tap once on the **Add to Favorites** button to add the contact to your favorites list, for quick access

7 Once you have selected a contact, FaceTime starts connecting to them and displays this at the top of the screen

8 When you have connected, your contact appears in the main window and you appear in a picture-in-picture thumbnail in the corner

Hot tip

The contacts for FaceTime calls are taken from the iPad Contacts app. You can also add new contacts directly to the contacts list by tapping once on the + sign and adding the relevant details for the new contact.

9 Tap once on this button to swap between cameras on your iPad

10 Tap once on this button to end the FaceTime call

11 If someone else makes a call to you, tap once on the **Decline** or **Accept** buttons

Messaging

Text messaging should not be thought of as the domain of the younger generation. On your iPad you can join the world of text with the Apple iMessage service that is accessed via the Messages app. This enables text and photo messages to be sent, free of charge, between users of the iOS 5, iOS 6 or iOS 7 operating systems, on the iPad, iPhone and iPod Touch. iMessages can be sent to cell/mobile phone numbers and email addresses. To use iMessages:

Beware

If a number, or an email address, is not recognized it shows up in red in the **To** box.

1 Tap once on the **Messages** app

2 Enter your Apple ID details and tap once on the **Sign in** button

3 Tap once on this button to create a new message and start a new conversation

4 Tap once on this button to select someone from your contacts

5 Tap once on a contact to select them as the recipient of the new message

Creating iMessages

To create and edit messages and conversations:

1 Tap once here and type with the keyboard to create a message. Tap once on the **Send** button

2 As the conversation progresses each message is displayed here

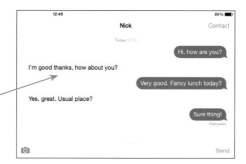

3 To edit whole conversations, tap once on the **Edit** button in the Messages panel

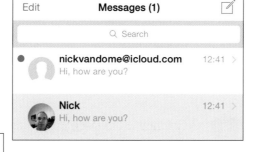

Edit

4 Tap once here and tap once on the **Delete** button to delete the conversation

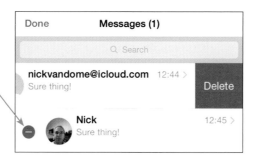

Hot tip

Press and hold on a message and tap on the **More** button that appears. Select a message, or messages, and tap on the **Trash** icon to remove them.

Don't forget

When a message has been sent you are notified underneath it if has been delivered.

Phoning with Skype

Skype is a popular app that is used on computers and mobile devices to make free phone and video calls. To do this, both users must have Skype installed on their computer or mobile device and have a microphone and speakers attached, either internally or externally.

As well as making free calls to other Skype users, it is also possible to phone standard telephone numbers and, although there is a charge for this, it is often cheaper than standard phone charges.

Downloading Skype

The Skype app is located within the **Social Networking** category of the App Store.

1　Access the App Store, enter **Skype** in the App Store Search box and tap once on the **Skype for iPad** link

2　Tap once here on the Skype app to download it

Using Skype

To make calls with Skype:

It is free to register for and join Skype.

1　Tap once on the **Skype** app

2　To use Skype you are required to register. This requires an email address and password

3　Enter your registration details and tap once on the **Sign In** button

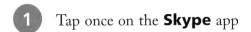

90

4 Tap once on this button to search for contacts or add a telephone number of someone you know

5 Contacts are added here

6 Tap once on a contact to make a call

Hot tip

Tap once on the button to the left of the **Add** button to access the number pad for entering phone numbers to call.

7 Tap once on the **Voice Call** button for a call

8 Tap once on **Video Call** button for a video call

9 Tap once on this button to mute the microphone

10 Tap once on this button to change the speaker volume

11 Tap once on this button to access the number pad for entering phone numbers

12 Tap once on this button to end a Skype call

Don't forget

If you find contacts via the search facility, they will be Skype users. Therefore, you will be able to contact them for voice or video calls free of charge.

91

Communication Apps

Within the App Store there is a range of communication apps that can be used to contact friends and family via text, phone and video. There are also several apps for sharing information, updates and photos. Some of these are:

- **Facebook.** The social networking phenomenon that has over a billion users around the world. This app enables you to create and use a Facebook account from your iPad. You can then interact with friends and family by posting messages, comments and photos.

- **Twitter.** Another of the top social networking sites on the Web. It provides the facility to post text or news messages of up to 140 characters. You can choose other users to follow, so you see their messages (tweets) and other people can follow you too.

- **Flickr.** An iPad version of the popular photo- and video-sharing site. You have to register and once you have done this you can share your photos and videos with a vast online community.

- **Pictures with Words.** Another photo-sharing app that enables you to share your photos online and also add captions, text and graphics to your images.

- **WordPress.** A web publishing app that can be used to create online blogs and also your own websites.

- **Gmail.** If you have a Gmail account this will enable you to access it directly from your iPad.

- **Windows Live Hotmail.** This can be used to access email from a Hotmail (or MSN or Live) account.

- **Yahoo! Messenger.** This app is similar to Skype in that it offers free video and voice calling to other Yahoo! Messenger users.

- **Talkatone for Google Voice and Facebook.** Another app for free phone calls and texts to phones in the USA and Canada.

Hot tip

On Facebook you can have private text conversations with your friends, as well as posting public information for all of your contacts to see.

Beware

When you follow people on Twitter, their tweets appear on your homepage. If they are very prolific, or you follow a lot of people, this may result in a lot of messages to read.

6 On a Web Safari

This chapter shows how to use the built-in iPad web browser, Safari, to access the Web and start enjoying the benefits of the online world.

94 Around Safari

96 Safari Settings

98 Navigating Pages

99 Opening New Tabs

100 Bookmarking Pages

101 Reading List and Shared Links

102 Web Apps

Around Safari

The Safari app is the default web browser on the iPad. This can be used to view web pages, save favorites and read pages with the Reader function. To start using Safari:

1 Tap once on the **Safari** app

2 Tap once on the Address Bar at the top of the Safari window. Type a web page address

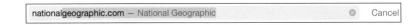
nationalgeographic.com — National Geographic   Cancel

3 Tap once on the **Go** button on the keyboard to open the web page

Go

4 Also, suggested options appear as you type. Tap once on one of these to go to that page

nationalgeographic.com — National Geographic
Top Hits
National Geographic
nationalgeographic.com
National Geographic - Kids
nationalgeographic.com/kids/
Google Search
national

5 The selected web page opens in Safari

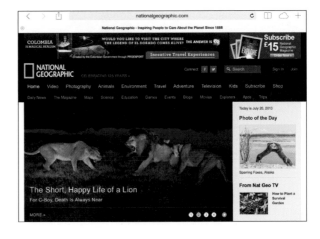

Don't forget

When a page opens in Safari a blue status bar underneath the page name indicates the progress of the loading page.

Apple

6 Swipe up and down and left and right to navigate around the page

7 Swipe outwards with thumb and forefinger to zoom in on a web page (pinch inwards to zoom back out)

Double-tap with one finger to zoom in on a page by a set amount. Double-tap with one finger to return to normal view. If the page has been zoomed by a greater amount by pinching, double-tap with two fingers to return to normal view.

Tap once on this button on the toolbar to access any web pages that are open in Safari on other Mac devices that you have, such as an iPhone, iMac or MacBook.

Safari Settings

Settings for Safari can be specified in the Settings app. To do this:

Don't use **Autofill** for names and passwords for any sites with sensitive information, such as banking sites, if other people have access to the iPad.

1 Tap once on the **Settings** app

2 Tap once on the **Safari** tab

3 Tap once on the **Search Engine** link to select a default search engine to use

GENERAL	
Search Engine	Google >

4 Tap once on the default search engine you want to use with Safari

‹ Safari	Search Engine	
Google		✓
Yahoo!		
Bing		

If the **Open New Tabs in Background** is set to On, you can tap and hold on a link on a web page and select **Open in New Tab**. The link then opens in a new tab behind the one you are viewing so as not to interrupt what you are doing.

5 Tap once here for options for filling in online forms

Passwords & AutoFill	>

6 Drag this button to On to open new pages in the background of your current page

Open New Tabs in Background	⬭

7 Drag this button to On to keep the Favorites Bar in view under the Address Bar in Safari

Show Favorites Bar	⬭

8 Drag the **Do Not Track** button to Off to disable this. If tracking is Off then no information will be recorded about visited websites

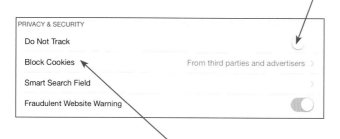

PRIVACY & SECURITY	
Do Not Track	
Block Cookies	From third parties and advertisers ›
Smart Search Field	›
Fraudulent Website Warning	

9 Tap once on the **Block Cookies** link to specify how Safari deals with cookies from websites

10 Tap once on **Clear History** and **Clear Cookies and Data** to remove these items

Clear History

Clear Cookies and Data

11 Drag this button to On to enable alerts for when you have visited a fraudulent website

Fraudulent Website Warning

12 Drag this button to On to block pop-up messages

Block Pop-ups

Cookies are small items from websites that obtain details from your browser when you visit a site. The cookie remembers the details for the next time you visit the site.

If the **History** is cleared then there will be no record of any sites that have been visited.

JavaScript files provide additional functionality for some websites.

Navigating Pages

When you are viewing pages within Safari there are a number of functions that can be used:

Hot tip

Tap and hold on the **Forward** and **Back** buttons to view lists of previously-visited pages in these directions.

See page 100 for more on bookmarking.

Hot tip

If a web page has this button in the Address/ Search box it means that the page can be viewed with the **Reader** function. This displays the page as text only, without any of the accompanying design to distract from the content. Tap on the button so that it turns black to activate the Reader.

1 Tap once on these buttons to move forward and back between web pages that have been visited

2 Tap once here to view Bookmarked pages, Reading List pages and Shared Links

3 Tap once here to add a bookmark, add to a reading list, add an icon to your iPad Home screen, email a link to a page, tweet a page, send it to Facebook or print a page

4 Tap once here to add a new tab

5 Tap once on a link on a page to open it. Tap and hold to access additional options, to open in a new tab, add to a Reading List or copy the link

6 Tap and hold on an image and tap once on **Save Image** or **Copy**

Opening New Tabs

Safari supports tabbed browsing, which means that you can open separate pages within the same window and access them by tapping on each tab at the top of the page:

1 Tap once here to open a new tab for another page

2 Open a new page by entering a web address into the Address Bar, or tap on one of the thumbnails in the **Favorites** window

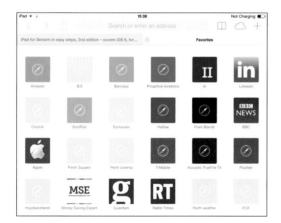

3 Tap once on the tab headings to move between tabbed pages

4 Tap once on the cross at the top of a tab to close it

Hot tip

The items that appear in the Favorites window can be determined within **Settings > Safari** and tapping once on the **Favorites** link.

NEW

Hot tip

If there are too many items to be displayed on the Favorites Bar, tap once on this button to view the other items.

Perth Squash   •••

Bookmarking Pages

Once you start using Safari you will soon build up a collection of favorite pages that you visit regularly. To access these quickly they can be bookmarked so that you can then go to them in one tap. To set up and use bookmarks:

Don't forget

The Favorites Bar appears underneath the Address Bar in Safari. This includes items that have been added as bookmarks.

1 Open a web page that you want to bookmark. Tap once here to access the sharing options

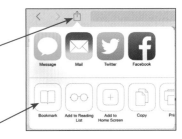

2 Tap once on the **Bookmark** button

3 Tap once on this link and select whether to include the bookmark on the Favorites Bar or in a Bookmarks folder

4 Tap once on the **Save** button

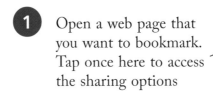
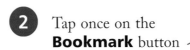
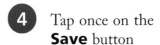

5 Tap once here to view all of the bookmarks. The Bookmarks folders are listed. Tap once on the **Edit** button to delete or rename the folders

Reading List and Shared Links

The button in Step 5 on the previous page can be used to access your Reading List and Shared Links.

Reading List
This is a list of web pages that have been saved for reading at a later date. The great thing about this function is that the pages can be read even when you are offline and not connected to the Internet.

Reading List items can be added from the Share button in Step 1 on the previous page.

Tap on this button to view your **Reading List**

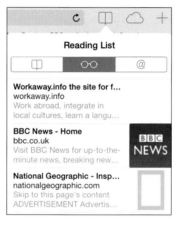

Shared Links
If you have added a Twitter account on your iPad you will be able to view your updates from the Shared Links button.

Tap on this button to view your **Shared Links** updates

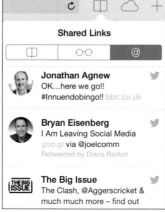
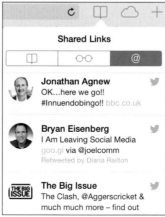

If you have accounts with Facebook or Twitter, you can link to these from the left-hand panel of the **Settings** app. Once you have done this you can share content to these sites from apps on your iPad.

Web Apps

Although Safari can comfortably meet all of your web browsing needs, there are a number of other browser apps that can be downloaded from the App Store. Generally, they have similar functionality but each has its own features too. It is worth looking at a few to compare the different interfaces. Some to try are:

- **Atomic Web Browser.** This is a browser that has a full-screen view, one-touch tabbed browsing and also a wider range of Multi-Touch Gestures for navigating.

- **Dolphin Browser.** This browser has four different search engines from which to choose and Gestures and Sidebars for accessing pages quickly.

- **Mercury Browser.** A stylish browser which includes customizable themes, ten-tab browsing, full-screen view and effective download options for links or images.

- **Opera Mini Web Browser.** This is a fast browser that compresses data before downloading it for viewing. One of the fastest browsers available for the iPad.

Beware

Flash is a video and animation format that is used widely on the Web. However, Flash video files cannot usually be played on the iPad.

- **SkyFire Web Browser.** This is an iPad browser with the unique feature of being able to play Flash video files. It does this by processing the content on its own servers and then sending it back to the browser. It is invaluable if you want to watch a lot of Flash video.

7 Staying Organized

An iPad is ideal for all of your organizational needs. This chapter shows how to keep notes, use address books and calendars, and set reminders and notifications. It also details some productivity apps.

104 Taking Notes

106 Setting Reminders

108 Using the Calendar

110 Your iPad Address Book

111 Keeping Notified

112 Viewing Notifications

113 Do Not Disturb

114 Organization Apps

115 Productivity Apps

116 Saving Documents

118 Printing Items

Taking Notes

It is always useful to have a quick way of making notes of everyday things, such as shopping lists, recipes or packing lists for traveling. On your iPad the Notes app is perfect for this function. To use it:

1 Tap once on the **Notes** app

2 Tap once on the note to access the keyboard. Start writing the note

Don't forget

Text in a note can be edited in the same way as any other text document.

104

3 Tap once on this button on the keyboard to hide the keyboard and finish the note. To edit an existing note, tap once on the text and the keyboard will reappear

4 As the note is created it appears in the Notes panel. The most recent note is at the top and the first line of the note is the title. Tap once on a note to view it

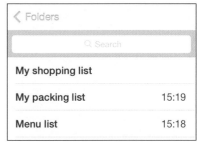

5 Tap once on this button to create a new note

6 Tap once on these buttons to, from left to right, delete a note; email, message or print a note, and move to the next note

Sending notes to iCloud

If you are using iCloud this can be used to send your notes to your iCloud account. To do this:

1 Access the Settings app and tap once on the **iCloud** link

2 Drag the **Notes** button to On

3 In the Notes app, tap once on the **Accounts** button

4 Tap on the links to view the notes in those categories

If iCloud is set up for Notes then all of your notes will appear under the **All iCloud** heading. If not they will all appear in the **On My iPad** account. Once in a specific account each note stays there, where it was created.

Setting Reminders

Another useful organization app is Reminders. This enables you to create lists for different topics and then set reminders for specific items. A date and time can be set for each reminder and, when this is reached, the reminder appears on your iPad screen. To use Reminders:

Reminders are one of the items that can also be viewed through the online iCloud service, which is provided once you have an Apple ID. This is accessed at **www.icloud.com** The other items that can be accessed there include Contacts, Calendar and Notes.

1 Tap once on **Reminders** app

2 The Reminder lists are located in the left-hand panel. Tap once on a list name

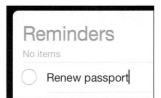

3 Tap once on a new line and enter the reminder

4 Hide the keyboard and tap once on the **i** button to access the **Details** window

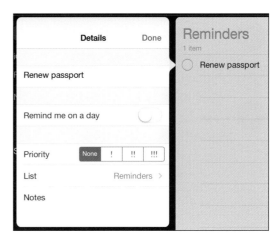

5 Drag this button to On

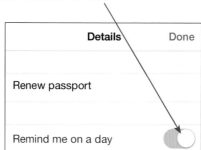

6 Tap once on the date and select a time and date for when you want the reminder alert

7 Tap once on the **Done** button

Done

8 At the date and time of the reminder, a popup box appears

9 Tap once on the **View Reminder** button to see the details of the reminder

For a recurring reminder, tap once on the **Repeat** link in the Details window (if **Remind me on a day is On**) and select a repeat option from None, Every Day, Every Week, Every 2 Weeks, Every Month, Every Year. The reminder will then appear at the specified timescale, at the time set in Step 6.

Set the time and date for reminders by dragging up and down on the relevant barrels within the **Details** window. The time can be set in five-minute intervals.

Using the Calendar

The built-in iPad Calendar can be used to create and view appointments and events. To do this:

1 Tap once on the **Calendar** app

2 By default the calendar is displayed in a month view. Swipe up and down to move between the weeks and months

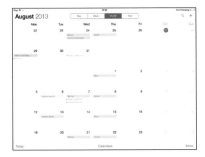

3 Tap once here to view the calendar by Day, Week, Month or Year view. Swipe left or right to move between days, weeks, months or years

4 Tap once on the **Today** button to view the current date. Tap once on the bar to move between dates

5 Tap once on this button to create a new event

6 Enter a Title and a Location for the event

7 Drag the **All-day** button to On to set a timescale for the event

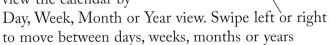

Cancel	Add Event	Done
80th Party		
Edinburgh		
All-day		
Starts	27 Jul 2013	17:00
Ends		18:00

108

8 Tap on the **Starts** and **Ends** dates to set these. Tap once on the **Done** button

9 To invite other people to the event, tap once on the **Invitees** link (Calendars needs to be On in iCloud for this function)

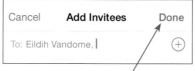

10 Tap once on this button to select a contact from your address book

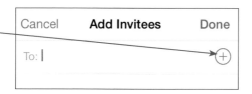

11 The contact is added as an invitee for the event

12 Tap once on the **Done** button. An email invitation will then be sent to the recipient's email address

13 Press and hold on an event and tap on the **Edit** button to alter the details for the event

Hot tip

A new event can also be created in **Day** view. Tap and hold on a time slot to access the **Add Event** window.

Hot tip

Tap once on the **Repeat** link in the **Add Event** window to set a recurring event, such as a birthday. The repeat options are Every Day, Every Week, Every 2 Weeks, Every Month or Every Year.

Don't forget

Swipe to the bottom of the **Edit** window to remove an event with the **Delete Event** button.

Your iPad Address Book

There is a built-in address book app on your iPad: Contacts. This enables you to store contact details which can then be used to contact people via email, iMessage or FaceTime. To add contacts:

1 Tap once on the **Contacts** app

2 Tap once on this button to add a new contact

3 Enter the required details for a contact

4 Tap once on the **Done** button

Done

5 Use these buttons to contact via text message (iMessage), video chat (FaceTime), share their contact details or add to your favorite contacts

Send Message

Share Contact

Add to Favorites

6 Tap once on the **Edit** button to edit details in an individual entry

Edit

7 To delete a contact, swipe to the bottom of the window in Edit mode and tap once on the **Delete Contact** button

Delete Contact

Hot tip

Tap once on a contact's email address to go directly to Mail to send them an email. Tap once on a cell/mobile phone number to access FaceTime for a video call (if the recipient has a compatible device and software for this).

Don't forget

Contact details of an individual can be shared via email or as an iMessage.

Keeping Notified

Although the Notification Center feature is not an app in its own right, it can be used to display information from a variety of apps. These appear as a list for all of the items you want to be reminded about or be made aware of. Notifications are set up within the Settings app. To do this:

1 Tap once on the **Settings** app

Tap once on the **Notification Center** tab

Drag the **Notifications View** and **Today View** buttons to On under the **Access on Lock Screen** heading. This will enable these items to be viewed even when the iPad is locked

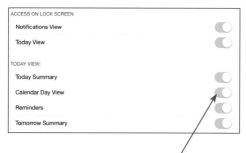

Drag the buttons to On for the items you want in the **Today View** of the Notification Center

Tap once on the items under the **Include** section to add items to appear in the Notification Center, under the **All** heading

Viewing Notifications

Once the Notification Center settings have been selected, it can be used to keep up-to-date with all of your important appointments and reminders. It can also be used to display the weather for your current location. To view the Notification Center from any screen:

1 Drag down from the top of any screen to view the Notification Center. Tap on the **Today** button to view the Weather summary, Calendar, items, Reminder items, and a summary of items for the next day

Press and hold on this button and swipe up to close the Notification Center:

2 Swipe up the page to view all of the items. Tap on one to open it in its own default app

3 Tap on the **All** button to view notifications from all of the selected apps in Step 4 on the previous page

All

4 Tap on the **Missed** button to view notifications that have not been actioned in any way

Missed

Do Not Disturb

Although Notifications can be set so that you never miss a new message or alert, there may be times when you do not want to receive any calls or audio alerts. This can be done with the Do Not Disturb function.

1 Tap once on the **Settings** app

2 Tap once on the **Do Not Disturb** tab

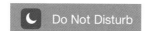

3 Drag the **Scheduled** button On, to specify a time period for when you do not want to be disturbed

4 Tap once on the **Allow Calls From** link to specify exceptions to Do Not Disturb

5 Select options for allowing calls (Favorites can be set for contacts in the Contacts app)

6 When Do Not Disturb is activated, a half-moon appears at the top of the screen next to the time

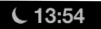

The Do Not Disturb feature stops video FaceTime calls and also any audio alerts that have been specified in the **Sounds** section of the **Settings** app.

Activate the **Repeated Calls** option so that people can still contact you in an emergency, by placing successive FaceTime calls, separated by less than three minutes.

Organization Apps

In the App Store there is a wide range of organization apps for tasks such as note-taking. Some of these are:

- **Evernote.** One of the most popular note-taking apps. You can create individual notes and also save them into notebook folders. Evernote works across multiple devices so, if it is installed on other computers or mobile devices, you can access your notes wherever you are.

- **Popplet.** This is an note-taking app that enables you to link notes together, so you can form a mindmap-type creation. You can also include photos and draw pictures.

- **Dropbox.** This is an online service for storing and accessing files. You can upload files from your iPad and then access them from other devices with an Internet connection.

- **Bamboo Paper.** This is another note-taking app, but it allows you to do this by handwriting rather than typing. The free version comes with one notebook into which you can put your notes and the paid-for version provides another 20.

- **Errands To-Do List.** A virtual To-Do list that can help keep you organized and up-to-date. You can create your own folders for different items and have alerts remind you of important dates, events and items.

- **Notability.** Another app that utilizes handwriting for creating notes. It also accommodates word processing, and audio recording.

- **Alarmed.** An app for keeping you on time and up-to-date. It has an alarm clock, pop-up reminders and pop-up timers.

- **Grocery List.** Shopping need never be the same again with this virtual shopping list app.

- **World Calendar.** Find out public holiday information for 40 countries around the world.

Don't forget

Most organization apps are found in the **Productivity** category of the App Store.

114

Beware

For handwriting to work most effectively in Bamboo Paper, **Multitasking Gestures** should be turned Off in the **General** section of the **Settings** app.

Productivity Apps

If you want to do more than just use organization apps, there are some excellent productivity apps for creating word processing documents, presentations and spreadsheets. These can be used to write letters, produce holiday presentations or do household accounts. Some of the productivity apps are:

- **Pages.** This is a powerful word processing app that has been developed by Apple. It can be used to create and save documents which can then be printed or shared via email. There are a number of templates on which documents can be based. There is also a range of formatting and content options.

- **Keynote.** Another Apple productivity app, this is a presentation app that can be used to create slides that can then be run as a presentation.

- **Numbers.** This is the spreadsheet app that is part of the same suite as Pages and Keynote. Again, templates are provided or you can create your spreadsheets from scratch to keep track of expenditure or household bills. You can enter formulas into cells to perform simple, or complicated, calculations.

- **Smart Office 2.** This app can be used to create, edit and share Microsoft Office documents, such as Word, Powerpoint and Excel. It supports all Microsoft Office versions since 1997 and also allows viewing of a variety of image files and PDF files.

- **iA Writer.** A simple but effective word processing app. It creates documents that can be synchronized across other devices and also copied to iCloud or Dropbox.

- **Free Spreadsheet.** This is similar to Numbers and although it does not have the same range of functionality it is still an effective spreadsheet.

- **GoodReader for iPad.** This is an app for viewing PDF documents and large documents such as manuals or long books. It also has a facility for annotating items.

Pages, Keynote and Numbers are part of Apple's iWork suite of productivity apps. They are all paid-for apps but still inexpensive and excellent value for money in terms of what they deliver.

PDF stands for Portable Document Format which is a file format created by Adobe to enable documents to be shared across different platforms without losing their formatting.

Saving Documents

For anyone who has grown up with computers and is used to a clear file structure, the first question when faced with an iPad is sometimes, 'Where do I save things?'. Unlike a Windows PC with Windows Explorer, or a Mac with the Finder, there is no obvious place to save files or create folders for content. This is because there isn't one. So where do you save your letters, presentations or photos once they have been created?

Self-contained saving

Instead of having a separate structure into which you can save files, content is saved within the apps in which they are created. So if you write a letter with the Pages word processing app, this is where is will be saved, and similarly if you create a note within the Notes app. Documents can be viewed as follows (this is for Pages):

Hot tip

iPad apps save content automatically as it is being created so you do not have to remember to keep saving it as you work.

1 Tap once on the Documents button **Documents**

2 All saved documents can be viewed here

3 When new documents are created they are added to this section. This is essentially the top-level folder

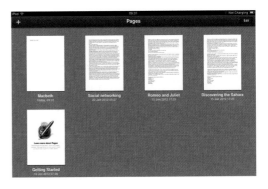

Adding folders

Despite the lack of a folder structure within the iPad operating system, folders can be created within some productivity apps, such as Pages. To do this:

1 Tap and hold on a document until it starts to jiggle. Drag it over another document icon

2 The new folder is created. Tap once here to give it a relevant name, then tap anywhere outside the folder to finish, or tap once on Done on the keyboard

You cannot create sub-folders, i.e. folders within folders. So the folder structure can only go down one level and you cannot copy one folder into another one.

3 The new folder appears in the main document area next to existing files

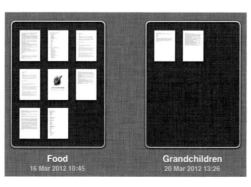

Printing Items

Printing from an iPad has advantages and disadvantages. The advantage is that it is done wirelessly so you do not have to worry about connecting wires and cables to a printer. The disadvantage is that not all printers work with the iPad printing system.

AirPrint

Content from an iPad is printed using the AirPrint system that is part of the iOS 7 operating system. This is a wireless printing system that connects to your printer through your Wi-Fi network. However, not all printers are AirPrint-enabled so it may not work with your current printer.

AirPrint can print content from Safari, Mail, Photos, Pages, Keynote, Numbers and PDF documents in iBooks. Some third-party apps have AirPrint facilities but this depends on individual developers. To print items using AirPrint:

Don't forget

Check on the Apple website for a list of AirPrint-enabled printers.

Beware

Some developers offer third-party printing apps for the iPad. However, these work with varying degrees of success.

1 Tap once on the tools option and select one of the Print options

2 Tap once on the **Print** link

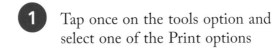

3 Select a printer or, if it has already been set up, tap once on the **Print** button to print

4 If your printer is not AirPrint compatible this will be shown in the **Printer** dialog box

8 Like a Good Book

This chapter looks at reading material on your iPad.

120 Newspapers and Magazines

122 Finding Books

126 Reading Books

130 Kindle on your iPad

Newspapers and Magazines

With its portability and high-resolution Retina screen, the iPad is ideal for reading material, from magazines and newspapers to books. The former can be downloaded and read with the Newsstand app and the latter with the iBooks app. To access reading material with the Newsstand:

Don't forget

There is a wide range of newspapers available through the Newsstand, usually specific to your geographical location.

1 Tap once on the **Newsstand** app

2 The Newsstand bookcase is initially empty. Tap once on the **Store** button to access the Newsstand store

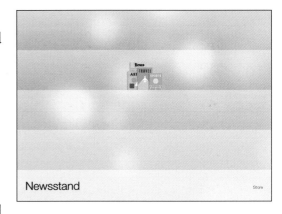

3 The Newsstand Store is incorporated within the App Store. Items can be found in the main featured panel or by swiping left and right between items underneath the top panel

Beware

The majority of magazines and newspapers are initially free to download. However, most then require a paid-for subscription once the initial trial period for the item has expired.

4 When you have found a suitable magazine, newspaper or journal, review and download it in the same way as with an app in the App Store

5 Downloaded items appear on the Newsstand bookcase (Library). Tap once on a cover to open that publication

If there is a red circle with a number in it on the Newsstand app, this indicates available updates for your existing publications.

Finding Books

For anyone interested in reading, the iPad removes the need to carry around a lot of bulky books. Whether you are at home or traveling, you can keep hundreds of books on your iPad. This is done with the iBooks app, which can be used to download and read books across most genres; it is your own portable library. To use iBooks:

1 Access the iBooks app in the App Store and download it in the same way as any other app

2 Tap once on this button once the **iBooks** app has been downloaded

Hot tip

Tap once on the **Collections** button to create new shelves under specific headings. These can be used to store books according to genre. Swipe left and right to move between collections.

3 The iBooks app interface consists of a bookcase, which initially is empty. Tap once on the **Store** button to access the iBooks store

4 Navigate through the iBooks Store in the same way as the App Store to find the required titles

5 Use these buttons to search for items within the iBooks Store

Looking for books

The buttons at the bottom of the iBooks window can be used to look for books in different ways:

1 Tap once on the **Top Charts** button to view the top selling books, for both paid-for and free books

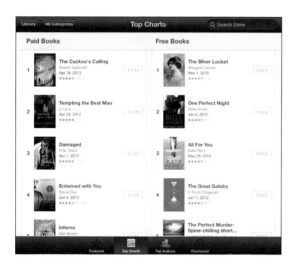

Hot tip

A lot of classic books can be downloaded for free, as their copyrights have expired.

123

2 Tap once on the **All Categories** button to view different categories of books. Tap once on a category to view all of the books within it

...cont'd

3 Tap once on the **Top Authors** button to look for books by author. Tap once on an author's name to see their available titles and editions

Next to the Top Authors title, tap once on the **Paid** or **Free** buttons, to view authors and books for these criteria.

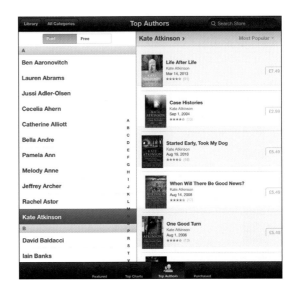

4 Tap once on the **Purchased** button to view the books that you have already downloaded or bought

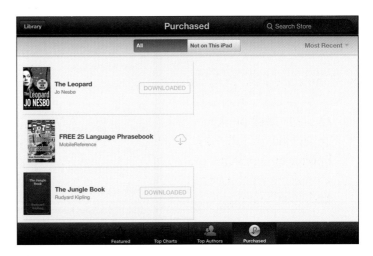

Downloading books

Once you have identified appropriate books they can then be downloaded to the iBooks bookcase (library). To do this:

1 Tap once on the book name or title to view its details

2 View the details of the book and any reviews (under the **Reviews** heading)

Under the **Related** heading in Step 2 you will find details of similar books to the one being viewed.

125

3 Tap once on this button to download a sample of the book

SAMPLE

4 Tap once here to download the book

£4.99

5 Downloaded books appear on the iBooks bookcase. Tap once on a book cover to open it and start reading

Reading Books

Reading an iBook

Once you have opened an iBook there are a number of ways to navigate and work with the content:

Hot tip

To hide the toolbar, tap once on a page.

1 Tap once in the middle of a page in an iBook to access the top toolbar

2 Tap once on this button to return to the iBook **Library** (bookcase)

3 Tap once on this button to view the Table of Contents

Don't forget

From the Table of Contents, tap once on the **Resume** button to return to the page you were looking at.

4 Tap once on this button to change the text size

5 Tap once on this button to search for an item in the book

Don't forget

If you are viewing a sample version of a book, there is a **Buy** button on the top toolbar. Tap once on this to buy the full version of the book.

6 Tap once on this button to bookmark a page

7 Drag on this bottom bar to move through the book

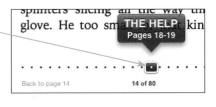

Working with text

When you are reading an iBook there are a number of options for enhancing the reading experience, from looking up dictionary definitions of words, to making notes about the text. To do this:

1 Tap and hold on a word to highlight it and access the text toolbar

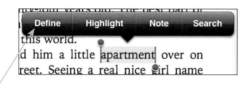

2 Tap once on the **Define** button to access a dictionary definition for the selected word. At the bottom of the window there are also options for searching the word over the Web or Wikipedia

Beware

If you use the Search Web or Search Wikipedia option, this takes you away from the iBook page.

3 Highlight a word and drag on the blue dots to extend the highlighted area

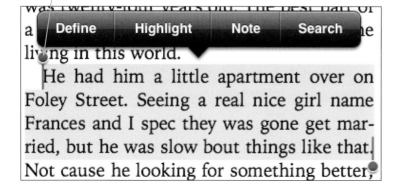

...cont'd

4 Tap once on the **Highlight** button and select an option for how the text is highlighted

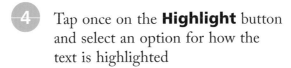

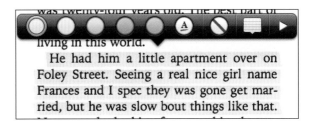

Beware

The more words you highlight for a search, the fewer results will be returned.

5 Highlight a word and tap on the **Search** button

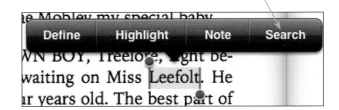

6 The Search results show where the highlighted word appears in the book. Tap one of the instances to go to that section in the book

7 Highlight a word or phrase and tap once on the **Note** button

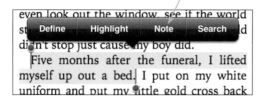

8 Enter your own note for the selected item

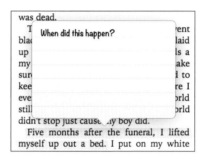

9 On the Table of Contents page, tap once on the **Bookmarks** button to view all of the bookmarked pages. Tap once on an item to view it

10 On the Table of Contents page, tap once on the **Notes** button to view all of the notes you have made in the book

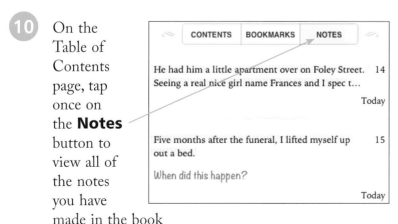

Kindle on your iPad

The Kindle is the most popular eReader device for reading eBooks. However, it is now possible to use the Kindle app on your iPad. If you already have a Kindle account, on Amazon, then you can also import books that you have downloaded to your iPad. To use Kindle on your iPad:

1 Download the Kindle app from the Books category in the App Store

2 Tap once on this button to open the **Kindle** app

3 If you have a Kindle account, enter the details here to register your iPad Kindle. Tap once on the **Register this Kindle** button

4 Tap once on this button to view the titles that are in the Kindle Cloud, i.e. have been downloaded to your Kindle account on Amazon

5 Tap once on this button to download a title from the Cloud to your iPad

6 Tap once on the **Device** button to view items that have been downloaded to your iPad

Beware

If you download a book from the Kindle Cloud it only appears under the **Device** button and not in your iBooks app.

7 Tap once on this button to view your books in list or icon view

8 Tap once on this button to sort your books by Most Recent, Title or Author

9 Tap once on this button to access **Settings** and other options for your Kindle on your iPad

...cont'd

Reading on the Kindle app

When you are reading a book on the Kindle app the options for navigating are similar to those for reading an iBook:

1 Tap once on this button to return to the main **Library** homepage

2 Tap once in the top right-hand corner of a page to add a bookmark

3 Drag on this button to move through the book

Tap once in the middle of a page to show or hide the toolbars.

4 Tap once on this button on the top toolbar to view options for the way the page is displayed. This includes text size and options for viewing black on white, white on black or sepia tone paper effect

5 If you are also reading books on a Kindle, tap once on this button on the bottom toolbar to synchronize your iPad version of the book with the Kindle one

9 Leisure Time

The possibilities for enjoying yourself with your iPad are huge. This chapter looks at downloading and listening to music and capturing and using photos and videos in different creative ways. It also covers some lifestyle opportunities and shows how you can obtain apps for viewing art, drawing, health, cookery and playing a range of games.

134 Buying Music

135 Playing Music

136 Using the Camera

138 Viewing Photos

140 Creating Albums

141 Selecting Photos

142 Sharing Photos

144 Editing Photos

146 In the Photo Booth

147 Capturing Videos

148 Viewing Videos

149 Photo and Video Apps

150 Discovering Art

151 Creating Pictures

152 Cooking with your iPad

153 Staying Healthy

154 Playing Games

Don't forget

If you have iTunes on another computer you can synchronize your music (and other items) that you have there to your iPad. To do this, attach the iPad to your computer (with the Dock Connector to USB Cable) and follow the setup instructions. You can check off the **Automatically Sync** options so that you can choose which items to sync. To manually update items, drag them from your iTunes Library over the iPad icon under **Devices**.

Buying Music

Music on the iPad can be downloaded and played using the iTunes and the Music apps respectively. iTunes links to the iTunes Store, from where music, and other content, can be bought and downloaded to your iPad. To do this:

1 Tap once on the **iTunes Store** app

2 Tap once on the **Music** button on the iTunes toolbar at the bottom of the window

3 Use these buttons at the top of the window to find music

| All Genres | Pop | Dance | Alternative | More |

4 Tap once on an item to view it. Tap once here to buy an album or tap on the button next to a song to buy that individual item

5 Purchased items are included in the Music app's Library

Playing Music

Once music has been bought on iTunes it can be played on your iPad using the Music app. To do this:

1 Tap once on the **Music** app

2 Use these buttons to find songs by different criteria

3 Tap once on a track to select it and start it playing

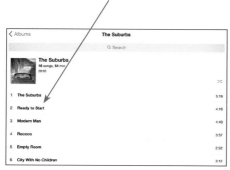

4 Tap once on the middle button to pause/play a selected song

5 Drag this button to increase or decrease the volume

6 Tap once on this button to repeat a song or album after it has played

Repeat

7 Tap once on this button to shuffle the order of songs

Shuffle

Music can also be played with the iTunes Radio service (only available in the US).

To create a Playlist of songs, tap once on the **Playlist** button, then tap once on the **New** button. Give it a name and then add songs from your Library.

Music controls, including Play, Fast Forward, Rewind and Volume can also be applied in the **Control Center**, which can be accessed by swiping up from the bottom of the screen.

Using the Camera

Because of its mobility and the quality of the screen, the iPad is excellent for taking and displaying photos. Photos can be captured directly using one of the two built-in cameras (one on the front and one on the back) and then viewed, edited and shared using the Photos app. To do this:

1 Tap once on the **Camera** app

2 Tap once on this button to capture a photo

3 Tap once on this button to swap between the front or back cameras on the iPad

Camera Settings
Certain camera options can be applied within Settings:

1 Tap once on the **Settings** app

2 Tap once on the **Photos & Camera** tab

3 Drag the **Photo Sharing**

button to On to enable sharing via a photo stream (see page 143)

4 Drag the **Grid** button

to On to place a grid over the screen, if required. This can be used to help compose photos by placing subjects using the grid

Don't forget

The camera on the back of the iPad is an iSight one and is capable of capturing high resolution photos and also high definition videos. The front-facing one is better for video calls.

Hot tip

Photos that are captured with the iPad camera are saved in the **Camera Roll** within the **Albums** section of the **Photos** app, as well as in the main Photos area.

Taking Photos

Photos taken with the camera on the iPad can be done in standard format or square format.

Beware

1 Swipe up or down at the side of the camera screen, underneath the shutter button. Tap once on the **Photo** button to capture photos at full screen size

Be careful to keep your fingers away from the camera lens when you are taking photos, particularly when you are using the camera on the other side of the iPad.

Hot tip

2 Swipe up or down at the side of the camera screen, underneath the shutter button. Tap once on the **Square** button to capture photos at this ratio

Tap once on the HDR (High Dynamic Range) button to take three versions of the same subject that will then be blended into a single photo, using the best exposures from each photo.

If you have iCloud set up, all of your photos will also be saved under the **My Photo Stream** button in the **Albums** section. This enables all of your photos to be made available on any other iCloud-enabled devices.

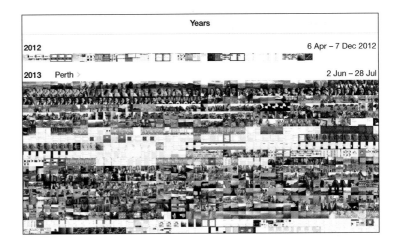

Tap once on the **Photos**, **Shared** and **Albums** buttons at the bottom of the **Years**, **Collections** or **Moments** windows, to view the photos in each of these sections.

Viewing Photos

Once photos have been captured they can be viewed and organized in the Photos app. To do this:

1 Tap once on the **Photos** app

2 At the top level, all photos are displayed according to the years in which they were taken

3 Tap once within the **Years** window to view photos according to specific, more defined, timescales. This is the **Collections** level. Tap once on the **Years** button to move back up one level

4 Tap once within the **Collections** window to drill down further into the photos, within the **Moments** window. Tap once on the **Collections** button to go back up one level

Don't forget

Moments are created according to the time at which the photos were added or taken: photos added at the same time will be displayed within the same Moment.

5 Tap once on a photo within the **Moments** window to view it at full size. Tap once on the **Moments** button to go back up one level

Hot tip

Double-tap with one finger on an individual photo to zoom in on it. Double-tap with one finger again to zoom back out. To zoom in to a greater degree, swipe outwards with thumb and forefinger.

6 Swipe with one finger or drag here to move through all of the available photos in a specific Moment

Don't forget

When photos are placed into albums the originals remain in the main **Photos** section.

Hot tip

Albums can be viewed as slideshows. To do this open the album and tap once on the **Slideshow** button.

Slideshow

Make the required selections and tap once on the **Start Slideshow** button.

Creating Albums

Within the Photo app it is possible to create different albums in which you can store photos. This can be a good way to organize them according to different categories and headings. To do this:

1 Tap once on the **Albums** button

Albums

2 Tap once on this button

3 Enter a name for the new album

New Album
Enter a name for this album.

Italy

Cancel   Save

4 Tap once on the **Save** button

5 Tap on the photos you want to include in the album

6 Tap once on the **Done** button

Done

7 Tap once on the **Done** button to finish creating the new album

Done

Italy

Selecting Photos

It is easy to take hundreds, or thousands, of digital photos and most of the time you will only want to use a selection of them. Within the Photos app it is possible to select individual photos so that you can share them, delete them or add them to albums.

1 Access the Moments section and tap once on **Select** button

Select

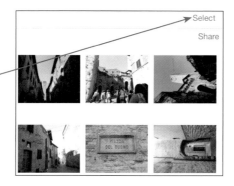

2 Tap on the photos you want to select, or tap once on the **Select** button again to select all of the photos

3 Tap once on the **Deselect** button if you want to remove the selection

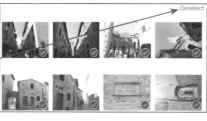

4 Use these buttons to, from left to right, share the selected photos, delete them or add them to an album

Hot tip

Press and hold on a photo to access an option to copy it, rather than selecting it.

Don't forget

To add items to an album, tap once on this button in the **Moments** section.

Select

Tap once on photos to select them, then tap once on the **Add To** button and select either an existing album or tap once on the **New Album** link to create a new album with the selected photos added to it.

Sharing Photos

Within the Photos app there are a number of ways to share and use photos. To do this:

1 Open a photo at full size and tap once on this button

2 Tap once on one of the options for sharing the photo. These include messaging, emailing, sending to iCloud, adding to a contact in your Contacts app, using as your iPad wallpaper, tweeting, sending to Facebook or Flickr, printing and copying the photo

Tweeting is done on the social networking site, Twitter.

Sharing Moments

Photo Moments can also be shared:

1 Access the **Moments** section and tap once on the **Share** button

2 Select **Share this moment** to share all of the photos in the moment, or **Share some photos** to make a selection

3 Select one of the sharing options (there may be fewer options when sharing multiple photos)

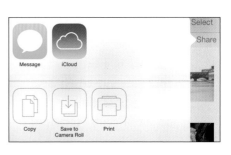

Sharing with Photo Stream

The Photo Stream option can be used to share photos with other people with the iCloud Photo Stream sharing function. To use this:

1 Select photos you want to share via Photo Stream and tap on the **Share** button

2 Tap once on the **iCloud** button

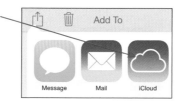

3 Enter a name for the new Photo Stream and tap once on the **Next** button

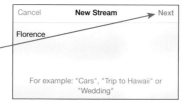

4 Enter a recipient with whom you want to share the Photo Stream and tap once on the **Create** button

5 Tap once on the **Next** button and enter a comment about the Photo Stream. Tap once on the **Post** button

Hot tip

Once a Photo Stream has been posted, the recipient receives an email inviting them to view it.

Editing Photos

The Photos app has options to perform some basic photo-editing operations. To use these:

1 Open a photo at full-screen size and tap once on the **Edit** button

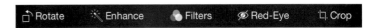

2 Tap once on the **Rotate** button to rotate the photo 90 degrees at a time, anti-clockwise

3 Tap once on the **Enhance** button to have auto-coloring editing applied to the photo

Don't forget

Use the Red-Eye editing option to remove red-eye for people by tapping once on the affected red-eye area.

Beware

Editing changes are made to the original photo once the changes have been saved. These will also apply to any albums into which the photo has been placed.

4 Tap once on the **Filters** button to select special effects to be applied to the photo

5 Tap once on the **Crop** button and drag the resizing handles to select an area of the photo that you want to keep and discard the rest

Most photos benefit from some cropping, to enhance the main subject and give it greater prominence.

6 For each function, tap once on the **Save** button to save the photo with the selected changes

7 Tap once on these buttons to, from left to right, cancel the whole editing process, undo the editing changes one step at a time, and remove all of the changes and go back to the original photo

In the Photo Booth

The Photo Booth app is one of the built-in iPad apps that can be used to create fun, creative photo effects. To use it:

1 Tap once on the **Photo Booth** app

2 The different special effects are shown through the camera. Tap once to select the desired effect

The Photo Booth app is a good one to use with grandchildren, who will enjoy experimenting with the special effects.

3 Check the image and capture it by tapping once on the camera shutter button

Capturing Videos

The iPad cameras can also be used to capture video, as well as photos. To do this:

1 Tap once on the **Camera** app

2 Swipe up or down so that the **Video** button is highlighted

3 Tap once on this button to swap cameras from front to back

4 Tap once on this button to record a video. Tap once on it again to stop recording

5 Once a video has been captured it is saved within the Photos app with the video camera icon and the duration of the video showing on the thumbnail. Tap once on this button to play a video

Video can take up a lot of storage space on your iPad. For instance, a one minute video takes up approximately 80MB of storage.

Viewing Videos

As the name suggests, the Videos app can be used to download and view video content. This is from the iTunes Store, rather than viewing your own videos. To do this:

Don't forget

The buttons at the top of the Films window can be used to search for films by All Genres, Action & Adventure, Classics, Comedy and the More option.

Don't forget

If you rent videos from the iTunes Store you have to watch them within 30 days. Once you have started watching the video you have to finish watching it within 48 hours. Once the rental period has expired, the video is deleted from your iPad.

1 Tap once on the **Videos** app

2 The Videos app is initially empty of content. Tap once on the **Store** button to access video content in the **iTunes Store**

3 Tap once on the **Films** button or the **TV** button

4 Tap once on an item to review its content. Tap once here to download it. This is usually in the form of buying or renting a video

5 The downloaded video appears in the Videos app. Tap once on the cover to view its contents

6 Tap once here to play a video

Photo and Video Apps

Within the App Store there is a category for Photo & Video, offering a range of apps for capturing and editing photos and videos. Some to try are:

- **iPhoto.** This is the iPad version of the popular Apple photo editing and organizing app. It is part of the iLife suite of apps and can be used as a photo library and also for a range of editing techniques, creating slideshows and sharing your photos.

- **Adobe Photoshop Express.** A mobile version of the bestselling Photoshop suite of video editing apps. Multi-Touch Gestures can be used to apply a range of editing techniques including artistic filters.

- **PowerCam HD.** A camera app that can be used to capture both photos and videos. Different special effects can be applied when the photos or videos are captured.

- **360 Panorama.** This is an app that can be used to stitch your photos together to create a 360 degree view.

- **Photo Collage HD.** An app for creating attractive collages with your photos. You can select and edit photos and add them to a collage with a range of backgrounds. It can then be shared via Facebook or Twitter.

- **iMovie.** Another app from the Apple iLife suite. This is used to edit video that you have captured. It offers functions to trim video, add transitions, captions, music and voiceovers. Once the video has been edited it can then be shared via YouTube, Facebook or iTunes.

- **Video Editor for FREE.** A video editing app that, as the name suggests, is free and a reasonable alternative to iMovie in terms of editing functionality.

- **Video Downloader.** A useful app that can be used to play most video formats through a browser interface.

- **Playable.** Another app for playing a wide range of video formats on your iPad.

Hot tip

The third app in the iLife suite is GarageBand. This is an app for creating your own music. It has a range of digital instruments that can be used to record tracks and also pre-recorded loops that can be added.

Discovering Art

It is always a pleasure to view works of art in real life, but the next best alternative is to be able to look at them on the high-resolution Retina display on your iPad. As far as viewing art goes, there are two options:

- Apps that contain general information about museums and art galleries.

- Apps that display the works belonging to museums and art galleries.

In general, type the name of a museum or art gallery into the App Store Search box to see if there is an applicable app. Some apps to look at are:

- **Guggenheim Bilbao.** Information and examples from the iconic museum in Bilbao.

- **London Museums.** A general guide for finding museums in London. With an Internet connection it can be used to phone museums for booking.

- **New York Museum Guide.** This is a comprehensive guide including opening hours, bookings and maps.

- **Musée du Louvre HD.** High-resolution images and descriptions of the world-famous art of the Louvre.

- **Museum Finder.** A general museum app for locating establishments around the world.

- **50 painting masterpieces you must see in Madrid.** A detailed guide to the Prado Museum in Madrid, including descriptions of 50 famous paintings.

- **Uffizi Touch.** Although this is more expensive than the other apps above, this offers a sumptuous tour of the works in the Uffizi Gallery in Florence.

Hot tip

If you cannot find a certain app under the **iPad Only** heading in the App Store, tap once on the button and select the **iPhone Only** option. These can be downloaded for the iPad too, although they will have a smaller screen area to view the app.

Hot tip

Most top museums have some form of app available. If there is not one for a museum in which you are interested try contacting the museum and asking if they are planning on developing an app.

Creating Pictures

If you want to branch out from just looking at works of art, you can try creating some of your own too. There is a range of drawing and painting apps that can be used to let your creative side run riot. Most of these function in a similar fashion in terms of creating pictures:

1 Drawing tools appear at the bottom of the app

2 Swipe from left to right to access different tool options and selections

3 Tap and draw with your finger on the screen to create a picture

151

You may find using a touch screen stylus makes drawing easier.

Some apps to try are:

- **Brushes.** One of the most powerful painting apps with a wide range of tools and features, including up to six layers in each painting and five blend modes.

- **Drawing Pad.** Similar to Brushes, but not at such a high level. Suitable as a first option for iPad painting.

- **Inspire Pro.** A wide range of blending features makes this one of the best painting apps around.

- **Learn to Draw.** A drawing app that has tutorials for learning how to draw and also examples that can be used as templates and copied over.

- **SketchBook Express.** A sketching app at a similar level to Brushes for painting.

Most drawing and painting apps have an **Undo** function and also an eraser that can be used to remove unwanted items.

Cooking with your iPad

Your iPad may not be quite clever enough to cook dinner for you, but there are enough cookery apps to ensure that you will never go without a good meal with your iPad at your side. Some to look at are:

Hot tip

If you are using your iPad in the kitchen, keep it away from direct contact with cooking areas, to avoid splashes. If there is a risk of this, cover the iPad with cling-film/plastic wrap to give it some protection.

152

- **AllRecipes.** Enter a type of food, or dish, into the search box and see a variety of related recipes.

- **BigOven 250,000+ Recipes.** As the name suggests, thousands of recipes to keep you busy in the kitchen for as long as you want. You can also store your grocery lists here.

- **Cake Recipes.** To get your mouth watering, this app has hundreds of cake ideas, from the simple to the exotic.

- **Green Kitchen.** A must for vegetarians, with stylish and creative recipes for organic and vegetarian food.

- **iCake Italian.** If you cannot make it to Italy, bring a bit of Italy to your home with these recipes for cakes, pastries and tiramisu.

- **Jamie's Recipes.** An app featuring the recipes of the well-known chef Jamie Oliver.

- **Recipes Starter Kit.** For the less experienced chefs, this is a good way to gain confidence in the kitchen.

- **Slow Cooker Recipes.** Put your dish together with this app, leave it in the slow cooker and then enjoy it several hours later when ready.

- **Sweet Baking.** As well as covering cakes and cookies this app also has recipes for a variety of breads.

Don't forget

Many recipe apps have a facility for uploading your own recipes, so that they can be shared with other people.

Staying Healthy

Most people are health conscious these days and the App Store has a category covering Health & Fitness. This includes apps about general fitness, healthy eating, relaxation and yoga. Some to try are:

- **Calorie Counter and Diet Tracker.** If you want to stick to a diet this app can help you along the way. You need to register, which is free, and then you can set your own diet plan and fitness profile.

- **Daily Workouts.** Some of the exercise apps are for dedicated gym-goers. If you are looking for something a bit less extreme this app could fit the bill. A range of exercises that will keep you fit without the need to be a body builder.

- **Daily Yoga.** Audio and video instructions for timed sessions and over 30 yoga poses.

- **Menu Planner.** A dieting aid that enables you to create your own menu plans.

- **MyPilatesGuru.** Use this app to work through over 80 pilates exercise sessions. You can also create your own sessions and save them to repeat.

- **Serenity.** Over 30 videos and sound files to help you relax or fall asleep.

- **Sleep Pillow Sounds.** Everyone enjoys a good night's sleep and this app can help you achieve it. A collection of ambient sounds are played to help you relax and sleep.

- **Universal Breathing.** Designed to promote slow breathing, to help with a range of health conditions including high blood pressure, migraines and asthma.

There is also a **Medical** category in the App Store that contains a range of apps covering medical topics and subjects.

153

If you have a genuine medical complaint, get it checked out by your doctor, rather than trying to find a solution through an app or on the Web.

Playing Games

Although computer games may seem like the preserve of the younger generation this is definitely not the case. Not all computer games are of the shoot-em-up or racing variety and the App Store also contains puzzles and versions of popular board games. There are two ways to access games:

- Via the App Store under the Games category.

- Via the Game Center built-in iPad app. This is usually used if you want to compare scores with other users or if you want to play games simultaneously with other people online in a multi-player game.

Some games to try are:

- **Chess.** Pit your wits against this chess app. Various settings can be applied for each game, such as the level of difficulty.

- **Checkers.** Similar to the Chess app, but for Checkers (Draughts). Hints are also available to help develop your skills and knowledge.

- **Mahjong.** A version of the popular Chinese game, but this is a matching game for single players, rather than playing with other people.

- **Scrabble.** An iPad version of the best-selling word game that can be played with up to four people.

- **Solitaire.** An old favorite, the card game where you have to build sequences and remove all of the cards.

- **Sudoku.** The numbers game where you have to fill different grids with numbers 1-9, without having any of the same in a row or column.

- **Tetris.** One of the original computer games, where you have to piece together falling shapes to make lines.

- **Words With Friends.** Similar to Scrabble, an online word game, played with other users.

Don't forget

As well as the games here, there is also a full range of other types of games in the App Store.

10 Getting on the Map

With an iPad, the Maps app and a Wi-Fi connection, the world is your oyster. This chapter shows how to find locations and directions.

156 Looking Around Maps

158 Finding Locations

159 Using Pins

160 Getting Directions

163 Finding Contacts

164 Types of Maps

165 Using Flyover

Looking Around Maps

With the Maps app you need never again wonder about where a location is, or worry about getting directions to somewhere. As long as you are connected to Wi-Fi you will be able to do the following:

- Search maps around the world
- Find addresses
- Find famous buildings or landmarks
- Find the locations of the people in your Contacts app
- Get directions between different locations
- View traffic conditions

To ensure that the Maps app works most effectively, it has to be enabled for Location Services so that it can use your current location. To do this:

Beware

You can view maps without enabling Location Services, but this means that Maps will not be able to use your current location, or determine anything in relation to this.

1 Tap once on the **Settings** app

Settings

2 Tap once on **Privacy** tab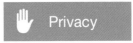

Privacy

3 Drag the **Location Services** and **Maps** button to On

Location Services

Location Services uses crowd-sourced Wi-Fi hotspot locations to determine your approximate location. About Location Services & Privacy...

Maps

Viewing maps

Once you have enabled Location Services you can start looking around maps:

1 Tap once on the **Maps** app

2 Tap once on this button to view your current location

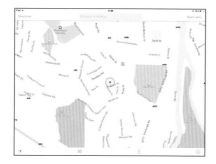

Tap on the icon in Step 2 to change it into the active compass, below. With this activated, when you change position, the map moves with you at the same time.

3 Double-tap with one finger on a map to zoom in

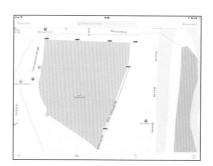

Don't forget

You can also zoom in and out on maps by swiping outwards with thumb and forefinger, or pinching inwards, respectively.

4 Tap once with two fingers on a map to zoom out

Finding Locations

Within Maps you can search for addresses, locations, landmarks, intersections or businesses. To do this:

1 Enter an item into the Search box

2 Tap once on the **Search** button on the keyboard

3 The required item is identified and shown on a map. Pins are also dropped at this point

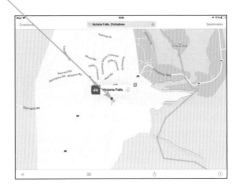

4 Locations can be viewed from a local, national or international level

Hot tip

You can also search for locations by postcodes or zip codes.

Using Pins

Pins are used to identify locations and also display additional information about locations or addresses. They can also be used to access photos for a location.

In addition to pins that are dropped when you find a location, you can also drop your own pins at any point. To use pins:

1 Tap once on a pin to view its options

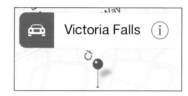

2 Tap once on this button to access additional information about the selected item

3 Tap once on the buttons under **Location** to add an item to your Contacts, or add to your Safari bookmarks, or share it via email, iMessage, Facebook or Twitter using the **Share** button

Tap on the **Directions** button on the pin options bar to find directions to the selected location.

4 To drop your own pin, tap and hold on a location. This drops a purple pin as opposed to the red ones. Tap and hold on a pin and drag it around to change its position

Getting Directions

Finding your way around is an important element of using maps and this can be done with the Directions function:

1 Tap once on the Directions button

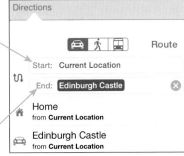

2 By default, your current direction is used for the **Start** field. If you want to change this, tap once and enter a new location or address

3 Enter a destination (**End**) location or address

4 Tap once on this button to swap the locations

5 Tap once on the **Route** button on the keyboard (or at the top of the Directions window)

Route

6 The route is shown on the map

7 Tap once on the **Start** button to get directions

8 The route is shown on the map with directions for each section

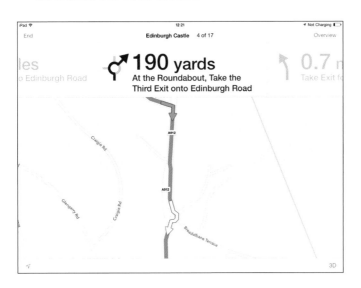

Hot tip

Depending on the directions, the map will be zoomed in and out as you access each instruction.

9 Swipe to the left and right to view the next, or previous, set of directions for the route

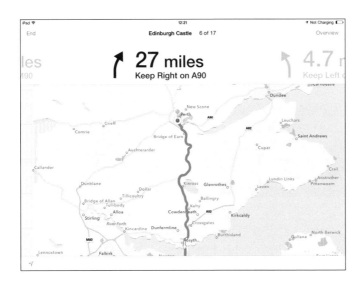

Don't forget

To get back to the Start view, tap once on the **End** button.

...cont'd

10 Tap once on this button in the bottom left-hand corner of the screen to view details of the route for the selected mode of transport. The default option is by car

Directions for public transport are not usually given between two destinations in different countries.

11 Tap once on this button and tap once on the **Route** button to find options via public transport

12 Tap on an app to download it for a specific mode of transport. This can then be used in conjunction with a route in the Maps app

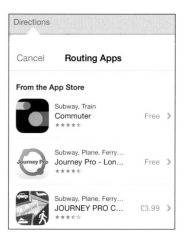

13 Tap once on this button to view the directions by foot

Finding Contacts

As well as looking for locations and landmarks, it is also possible to find locations and directions for people in your address book (Contacts app). To do this:

1   Tap once on the **Bookmarks** button   Bookmarks

2   Tap once on a contact in your Contacts app

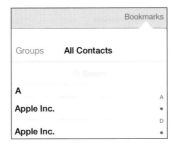

3   If the contact has more than one address, i.e. home and work, tap once on the one you want to view

4   The selected address is displayed on a map and a pin will be dropped at the address

Don't forget

If there is no address entered for a contact their name will be grayed-out in Step 2 and you will not be able to select them.

Don't forget

Tap once on the **i** button on the pin toolbar, to see a photo of the location.

Types of Maps

The standard view that is used in Maps can be changed so that you can view maps according to satellite and hybrid views. To do this:

Hybrid and Satellite maps can be zoomed in and out on, in the same way as for the Standard map view.

1 Tap here to access the map options

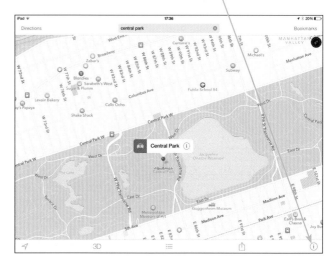

2 Tap on the buttons in the corner to select the map types (**Standard**, **Hybrid** and **Satellite**). Tap anywhere on the map to hide the options

Tap once on the **Show Traffic** button to show any traffic congestion on the map being viewed. Red markings indicate an average speed below 25mph; yellow, 25-50mph; and green, over 50mph.

Using Flyover

One of the innovative features in the Maps app is the Flyover function. This enables you to view locations in 3D relief, as if you were moving over them from above. You can also zoom in and change the perspective. To use Flyover:

1 Access a map and select the **Satellite** option

2 Tap once on this button to activate the Flyover functionality (if available for the area being viewed)

3 The perspective changes so you are viewing the map from an angle

Beware

The Flyover function is only available for certain cities around the world, with the majority being in the USA. However, this number is increasing regularly. If Flyover is not available, the button in Step 2 is 3D.

...cont'd

 Zoom and swipe to 'fly over' the map (zoom in by pinching together with thumb and forefinger)

Depending on the speed of your Internet connection, it may take a few seconds to render the map each time you move to the next view with Flyover.

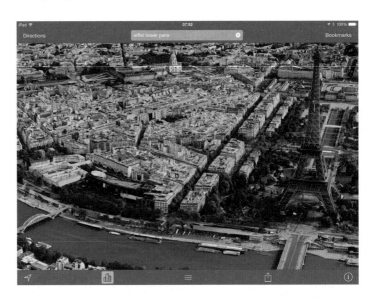 Swivel the map by turning in a circular fashion with thumb and forefinger, to view it from a different perspective

When viewing maps, the compass icon in the top right-hand corner indicates the direction of north.

11 Traveling Companion

This chapter shows why you should never be without your iPad when you are traveling or on vacation.

168 Traveling with your iPad

169 Planning your Trip

171 Viewing Flights

172 Finding Hotels

173 Converting Currency

174 Travel Apps

Traveling with your iPad

When you go traveling, there are a few essentials that you have to consider: passport, money and insurance to name three. To this you can add your iPad: it is a perfect traveling companion that can help you plan your trip and keep you informed and entertained when you are away from home.

Uses for traveling

There are a lot of App Store apps that can be used for different aspects of traveling. However, the built-in apps can also be put to good use before and during your travels:

The Clock app can also be used so that you can keep an eye on the time in different parts of the world.

- **Maps.** Use this app for accessing maps of your destinations, finding directions and viewing images of areas to which you are traveling.

- **Notes.** Create items such as lists of items to pack or landmarks that you want to visit.

- **Contacts.** Keep your Contacts app up-to-date so that you can use it to send postcards to friends and family. You can also use it to access phone numbers if you want to phone home.

- **Reminders.** Set reminders for important tasks, such as changing foreign currency, buying tickets and details of flights.

- **Music.** Use this app to play your favorite music while you are traveling, or relaxing at your destination.

- **Photos.** Store photos of your trip with this app and play them back as a slideshow when you get back home.

You can also use the Videos app to download movies and TV shows from the iTunes Store. However, these will take up a significant amount of space on your iPad in terms of storage.

- **FaceTime.** If you have a Wi-Fi connection at your destination you will be able to keep in touch with video calls (as long as the recipient has FaceTime too).

- **iBooks.** Instead of dragging lots of heavy books around, use this app for your vacation library.

Planning your Trip

A lot of the fun of going on vacation and traveling is in the planning. The anticipation of researching new places to visit and explore can whet the appetite for what is ahead. The good news is that you can plan your whole itinerary while sitting in an armchair with your iPad on your lap. In the App Store there are apps for organizing your itinerary and others for exploring the possibilities of where you can go:

Tripit

This is an app for keeping all of your travel details in one place. You have to register, which is free, and you can then enter your own itinerary details. Whenever you receive an email confirmation for a flight, hotel or car hire that you have booked, you can email this to your Tripit account (**plans@tripit.com**) and this will be added to your itinerary.

GetPacked

A great way to get peace of mind before you leave. This app generates a packing list and to-do lists to check before you leave, based on questions that you answer about your vacation and travel arrangements. You can then select items to include on your packing list, from clothes to documents and medical items.

Although there is a small fee for the GetPacked app, it is well worth it as it covers everything you will need to consider before you leave.

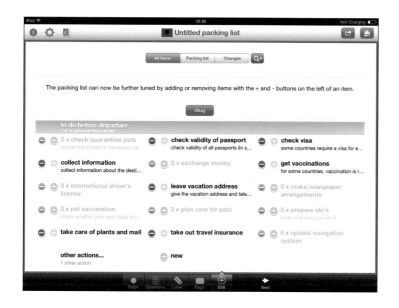

...cont'd

Cool Escapes

Guaranteed to give you itchy feet, this app matches quality hotels with some amazing locations around the world. You can explore by map, country, area, hotel type and price, to find the perfect combination.

World Travel Atlas

A comprehensive travel companion that offers a world atlas that contains information about countries, cities, landmarks, airports and events. Navigate around the atlas with the same swiping and tapping gestures as with the Maps app. Tap once on an item to access a wealth of information about it.

Beware

Some maps apps are free to download but there is then a fee to buy the associated maps.

Viewing Flights

Flying is a common part of modern life and although you do not have to book separate flights for a vacation (if it is part of a package) there are a number of apps for booking flights and also following the progress of those in the air:

Skyscanner
This app can be used to find flights at airports around the world. Enter your details such as leaving airport, destination and dates of travel. The results show a range of available options, covering different price ranges.

FlightRadar24
If you like viewing the path of flights that are in the air, or need to check if flights are going to be delayed, this app provides this inflight information. Flights are shown according to flight number and airline.

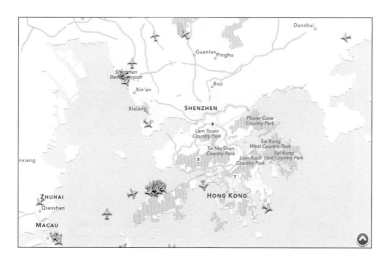

Flight apps need to have an Internet connection in order to show real-time flight information.

AirportZoom
As well as showing real-time flight details, this app also has airline departure and arrival information and maps of airport terminals and flight gates.

FlightAware
Another app for tracking flights, showing arrivals and departures and also information about delays.

Finding Hotels

The Internet is a perfect vehicle for finding good value hotel rooms around the world. When hotels have spare capacity, this can quickly be relayed to associated websites, where users can usually benefit from cheap prices and special offers. There are plenty of apps that have details of thousands of hotels around the world, such as:

TripAdvisor

One of the top travel apps, this not only has hotel information but also restaurants, activities and flights. Enter a destination in the search box and then navigate through the available options.

Hotels.com

A stylish app that enables you to enter search keywords or tap once on a hotel on the Home screen to view options for this location.

Hot tip

Most hotel apps have reviews of all of the listed establishments. It is always worth reading these as it gives you a view from the people who have actually been there.

Booking.com

Another good, fully-featured hotel app that provides a comprehensive service and excellent prices.

LateRooms.com

An app that specializes in getting the best prices by dealing with rooms that are available at short notice. Some genuine bargains can be found here, for hotels of all categories.

Converting Currency

Money is always important in life and never more so than when you are on vacation and possibly following a budget. It is therefore imperative to know the exchange rate of currencies in different countries compared to your own. Two apps that provide this service are:

XE Currency

This app delivers information about exchange rates for all major world currencies and also a wealth of background information such as high and low rates and historical charts.

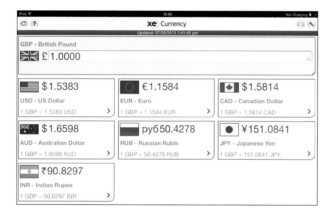

Currency

This app provides up-to-date exchange rates for over 150 currencies and 100 countries.

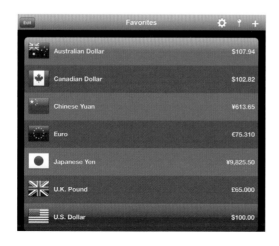

When changing currency, either at home or abroad, always shop around to get the best rate. Using credit cards abroad usually attracts a supplementary charge too.

Don't forget

Fotopedia has other photography apps, covering areas including National Parks, Wild Friends and Women of the World.

Travel Apps

Everyone has different priorities and preferences when they are on vacation. The following are some apps from the App Store that cover a range of activities and services:

- **1000 Places To See Before You Die.** A collection of stunning and unforgettable destinations and locations around the world. Impressive photography makes it all the more appealing and you can also browse maps.

- **Disneyland Paris.** If you are entertaining your grandchildren at Disneyland Paris, this app will help you survive the experience. Maps, show times and descriptions of features help you organize all aspects of your visit.

- **Fotopedia Heritage.** A selection of stunning photography of World Heritage sites. Guaranteed to make you want to head for the airport.

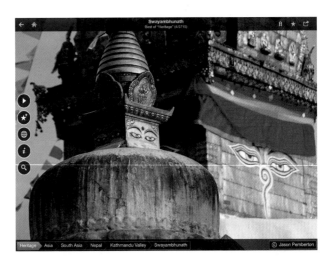

- **Florida Theme Parks.** Another one for the family and grandchildren. Everything you need to know about these popular tourist attractions.

- **Google Earth.** Not just a travel aid, this app enables you to search around the globe and look at photos and 3D maps of your favorite places.

- **Hailo.** For anyone visiting London, New York, Dublin, Toronto and other large cities (more being added), this app allows you to hail a cab, at the tap of a button.

- **Kayak.** A useful all-round app that compares hundreds of travel websites to get the best prices for flights, hotels and car rental. You can also create your own itineraries.

- **Language apps.** If you want to learn a new language for your travels, there is a wide range of apps for this. These are located in either the Travel or Education categories in the App Store.

- **Laplication.** For something a little bit off the beaten track, use this app to see the wonders of Lapland, including the incredible Northern Lights.

- **myLanguage Free Translator.** If you do not have the time, or inclination, to learn a new language, try this app to translate 59 different languages.

- **National Geographic Traveler.** Subscribe to this app to get an endless supply of high-quality travel features, photography and travel ideas.

- **New York Subway Map.** Use this app to help get around the Big Apple via the Subway. Plan your journeys and view live updates about stations and routes.

Don't forget

There are apps for displaying train times and details, but these are usually specific to your geographical location rather than covering a range of different countries.

175

...cont'd

- **Over 40 Magnifier and Flashlight.** Not just for traveling, this fantastic app acts as a torch and a magnifying glass all in one.

- **P&O Cruises.** Find some of your favorite cruises with this app that displays the full brochure of P&O Cruises.

- **Paris Transport Map.** One free map for travel options around one of the great cities in the world.

- **Photo Translator.** Ever wondered what signs in a foreign language mean? This app can translate them for you: take a photo with your iPad and the app gives you a translation of the sign, or phrase.

- **Phrasebook.** Keep up with what the locals are saying in different countries with this app that has useful phrases in 25 languages.

- **Sixt Rent a Car.** Use this app for car rental in 90 countries around the world.

- **London Tube Map.** Find your way around London with this digital version of the iconic Tube Map. It includes live departure boards and station information.

- **Urbanspoon.** Another app for finding restaurants on your vacation. Enter your location, shake your iPad and the app uses a slot machine interface to come up with suggestions. Covers USA, Canada, UK, Australia and New Zealand.

- **Weather+.** An app for showing the weather in locations around the world, including hourly updates.

- **Wi-Fi Finder.** It is always useful to be able to access Wi-Fi when you are on vacation, and sometimes essential. This app locates Wi-Fi hotspots in 650,000 locations in 144 countries worldwide.

- **Yelp.** Covering a range of services, this app locates restaurants, shops, services and places of interest in cities around the world.

Beware

The Phrasebook app comes with one free language. After that you have to pay a small fee for each language that you want to use.

12 Practical Matters

This chapter looks at security on the iPad and locating a lost device. It also shows how to use it for financial management and buying property.

178 Setting Restrictions

180 Finding your iPad

182 Locking your iPad

183 Avoiding Viruses

184 Dealing with Money

185 Looking at Property

186 Financial Apps

Setting Restrictions

Within the iPad Settings app there are options for restricting types of content that can be viewed and also actions that can be performed. These include:

- Turning off certain apps so that they cannot be used

- Enabling changes to certain functions

- Restricting content that is viewed using specific apps

When setting restrictions, they can be locked so that no-one else can change them. To set and lock restrictions:

Hot tip

It is a good idea to set up some restrictions on your iPad if grandchildren are going to have access to it.

1 Tap once on the **Settings** app

Settings

2 Tap once on the **General** tab

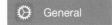

⚙ General

3 Tap once on the **Restrictions** link

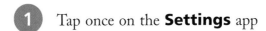

Restrictions   Off >

4 The restrictions are grayed-out, i.e. they have not been enabled for use yet

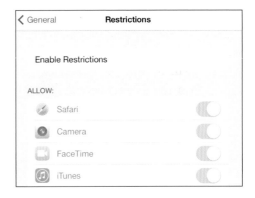

❮ General   **Restrictions**

Enable Restrictions

ALLOW:

🧭 Safari

📷 Camera

📹 FaceTime

🎵 iTunes

5 Tap once on the **Enable Restrictions** link

Enable Restrictions

6 Type on the keypad to set a passcode for enabling and disabling restrictions

7 Re-enter the passcode

If you forget the passcode for unlocking your iPad it will become disabled for a period of time after you have entered the wrong passcode a number of times. Eventually, it will lock completely. It can be reset by using a computer with which the iPad was last synced and there are details about this on the Apple website Support pages. However, to avoid this, ensure that you have a note of the iPad's passcode, but keep it away from the iPad.

8 All of the Restrictions options become available. Drag these buttons On or Off to disable certain apps. If this is done they will no longer be visible on the Home screen. Tap once on the links under **Allowed Content** to specify restrictions for certain types of content, such as music, movies, books and apps

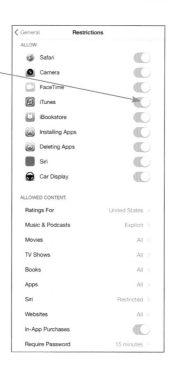

Finding your iPad

No-one likes to think the worst, but if your iPad is lost or stolen, help is at hand. The Find My iPad function (operated through the iCloud service) allows you to send a message and an alert to a lost iPad and also remotely lock it or even wipe its contents. This gives added peace of mind, knowing that even if your iPad is lost or stolen its contents will not necessarily be compromised. To set up Find My iPad:

1 Tap once on the **Settings** app

2 Tap once on the **iCloud** tab

3 Tap once on the Find My iPad link and drag the button to On to be able to find your iPad on a map

Find My iPad   Off >

4 Tap once on the **OK** button to enable the Find My iPad functionality

Find My iPad

This enables Find My iPad features, including the ability to show the location of this iPad on a map.

Cancel   OK

Hot tip

Location Services and **Find My iPad** both have to be turned On to enable this service. This can be done in the Settings app (**Settings > Privacy > Location Services > Find My iPad**).

Finding a lost iPad

Once you have set up Find My iPad you can search for it through the iCloud service. To do this:

1 Log in to your iCloud account at **www.icloud.com**

2 Tap once on the **Find My iPhone** button (this also works for the iPad)

3 Tap once on the **All Devices** button and select your iPad. It is identified and its current location is displayed on the map

4 Tap once on the green circle to view details about when your iPad was located

Don't forget

Click once on the **Erase iPad** button to delete the iPad's contents.

5 Tap once here to send a sound alert to your iPad

6 Tap once here to lock your iPad

7 Enter a passcode so that no-one else can access the contents on your iPad

Locking your iPad

As shown in Chapter Two, the screen can be auto-locked, but this does not have a security control. If you want to make sure that no-one else can access your iPad's content a passcode can be set for unlocking the screen. To do this:

Hot tip

In the **Passcode Lock** section you can allow access for Siri even when the iPad is locked, i.e. from the Lock screen.

Don't forget

Once the passcode has been set, tap once on the **Require Passcode** button to specify when the passcode is activated. This can be immediately, or over a period of time.

1 Tap once on the **Settings** app

2 Tap once on the **General** tab

3 Tap once on the **Passcode Lock** button

4 Tap once on the **Turn Passcode On** link

5 Enter the passcode and re-enter it to confirm it

6 The passcode has to be entered to access the iPad for use every time it has been locked

Avoiding Viruses

As far as security from viruses on the iPad is concerned there is good news and bad news:

- The good news is that, due to its architecture, most apps on the iPad do not communicate with each other so, even if there was a virus, it is unlikely that it would infect the whole iPad. Also, there are relatively few viruses being aimed at the iPad, particularly compared to those for Windows PCs.

- The bad news is that no computer system is immune from viruses and malware, and complacency is one of the biggest enemies of computer security. Also, as iPads become more popular they will become a more attractive target for hackers and virus writers.

iPad security

Apple takes security on the iPad very seriously and one way that this manifests itself is in the fact it is designed so that different apps do not talk to each other. This means that if there was a virus in an app then it would be hard for it to transfer to others and therefore spread across the iPad. Apple's own apps are the exception to this, but as they are developed and checked by Apple there is very little chance of them being infected by viruses.

Antivirus options

There are a few apps in the App Store that deal with antivirus issues, although not actually removing viruses. Some options to look at:

- **VirusBarrier.** This checks files that are copied onto your iPad, via email or online services, to ensure that they are virus-free.

- **McAfee Global Threat Intelligence Mobile.** This is not technically an antivirus app, but it does provide a daily update about new viruses that are in circulation.

- **Anti-Virus Detective.** This is an app that has a step-by-step process for identifying suspected viruses or malware.

Malware is short for malicious software, designed to harm your computer or access and distribute information from it.

Apple also checks apps that are provided through the App Store and this process is very robust. This does not mean that it is impossible for a virus to infect the iPad (but there have not been any so far) so keep an eye on the Apple website to see if there are any details about iPad viruses.

Dealing with Money

We all like to keep track of our money and, although it may not be as much fun as reading books or looking at photos, it is a necessary task that can be undertaken on the iPad.

Some general financial apps are looked at on page 186, but one of the most common uses for financial matters is online banking. This is where you can use banking apps to access your bank accounts.

Banking apps are specific to your geographical location, i.e. the banks that operate in your country. Most banking apps operate in a similar way:

Beware

If you are logging into your online banking service, make sure any Remember Me log in details functions are checked off, particularly if other people have access to your iPad.

Don't forget

Online banking sites can also be accessed through the Web using Safari.

1 You have to first register for the online service. Once you have done this, tap on the Log On button to access your account details

2 General information is also available through the app, such as branch locations and contact details

Looking at Property

If you are looking to move home, or buy property as an investment, your iPad is a great starting point. There are a lot of real estate apps that provide high quality color photos of all parts of properties for sale.

As with banking apps, real estate apps are specific to your geographical location and they all have a search facility for looking for properties in different areas. The search results can usually be filtered by criteria such as price, number of bedrooms and property type. To use a real estate app:

1. Browse properties according to area

Some property apps also allow you to book appointments to view properties in person.

2. Tap once on a property to view more details. This usually includes photos of all of the rooms and a full description of the property

Financial Apps

Within the Finance category of the App Store there are apps for managing your personal finances, viewing share prices and organizing your bank accounts and bills. Some to look at are:

- **Account Tracker.** A useful app for keeping track of your expenditure. It can be used to monitor multiple bank accounts and also set alerts and reminders for paying bills.

- **Calculator.** For working out your own finances, this calculator provides a large, attractive interface with plenty of functionality.

- **Bloomberg.** This is an app for following stocks and shares. You can add any shares that you own and view live prices while markets are open (with a 15 minute delay). There is also a financial news service.

- **HomeBudget.** An app for managing your household incomes and expenses. It also supports charts and graphs so you can compare expenditure over periods of time.

- **Meter Readings.** Useful for keeping an eye on your fuel consumption, this app helps you to save money by monitoring your utility readings. Enter the readings and your usage and costs are displayed in user-friendly graphs to show where savings can be made.

- **Mint.com.** Another general finance app for managing your money and monitoring budgets.

- **Money for iPad Free.** As well as being used to manage bills and view all of your accounts, this app also provides useful planning features and reminders.

- **Pocket Expense.** Another in the range of apps with which you can monitor bank accounts, track bills, view transactions and see where you can save money.

- **SharePrice.** Another app for seeing how your share portfolio is doing. Real-time share information, market news and profit/loss details are provided.

Hot tip

With your iPad and an Internet connection, you should always be able to keep an eye on your shares portfolio as well as buying and selling shares, wherever you are.

A

Accented letters	
Accessing	57
Accessibility	41-46
Guided Access	46
Hearing settings	43
Vision settings	42-43
Account Tracker	186
Address book	110
Adobe Photoshop Express	149
AirDrop	62
AirPlay Mirroring	11
AirPrint	118
Alarmed	114
Anti-Virus Detective	183
Antivirus options	183
Apple Digital AV Adapter	11
Apple ID	
Obtaining	79
Apple VGA Adapter	11
Apple Wireless Keyboard	48
Apps	8
Art	150
Built-in	
Camera	63
Closing	25
Communication	92
Cookery	152
Deleting	76
Downloading	72
Drawing	151
Explained	62
Financial	186
Finding	68-71
Searching for	71
Folders	75
Free	72
Geographic availability	68
Health & Fitness	153
In-app purchases	72
Language	175
Organization	114
Organizing	74-75
Photo	149
Price	72
Productivity	115-116
Travel	174-176
Updating	73
Video	149
Web	102
Apps (built-in)	
App Store	63
Calendar	63
Camera	63
Clock	63
Contacts	63
FaceTime	64
Game Center	64
iBooks	64
iTunes Store	64
Mail	64
Maps	64
Messages	64
Music	65
Newsstand	65
Notes	65
Photo Booth	65
Photos	65
Reminders	65
Safari	65
Settings	63
Videos	65
App Store	
About	66-67
Downloading apps	72
Finding apps	68-71
Near Me	70
Updating apps	73
Viewing apps	67
Art	
Viewing	150
AssistiveTouch	44-46
Atomic Web Browser	102
Auto-Correction	59
Auto-Locking	
The screen	39

B

Backgrounds
   With wallpaper 15
   With your own photos 15
Bamboo Paper 114
Battery power 11
Bloomberg 186
Books 122-129
   Bookmarking pages 126
   Downloading 125
   Finding 122-124
   Highlighting items 127
   Making notes 129
   Reading 126-129
   Searching within a book 128
   Using the dictionary 127

C

Calculator 186
Calendar 108-109
Camera 136
   Using 136-137
Cameras 12
Cellular settings 20
Charging. See iPad: Charging
Closing items 25
Connecting to a HDTV 11
Contacts 110
Control Center 26-27
Cooking 152

D

Dictation. See Voice typing
Disneyland Paris 174
Dock 22-23
   Adding and removing items 23
   Rearranging items 22
Dock cable connector 12

Documents
   Adding folders 117
   Saving 116-117
Dolphin Browser 102
Dragon Dictation 60
Dropbox 114

E

Email 80-84
   Creating 83
   Mailboxes 84
   Setting up an account 80-81
   Threads 81
   Viewing 82
   VIPs 84
Errands To-Do List 114
Evernote 114
Excel 115

F

Facebook 62, 85, 92, 101, 142
FaceTime
   For video chatting 86-87
Fetch New Data 82
Find My iPad 180-181
   Remote Wipe 181
Fitness 153
Flash video 102
Flickr 85, 92
Florida Theme Parks 174
Fotopedia Heritage 174
Fraud warnings
   On websites 97
Free Spreadsheet 115

G

Games 154
Game Center 154

GarageBand	149
Getting online	78
Gmail	92
GoodReader for iPad	115
Google Earth	174
Grocery List	114

H

Hailo	175
HDR	137
Health	153
HomeBudget	186
Home Button	16
Home Screen	15
Returning to	28

I

iA Writer	115
iBooks	122-129
iCloud	35-37
Backup	37
Settings	36
Storage	36, 37
iCloud Keychain	37
iLife	149
iMessages	88-89
Creating	89
iMovie	149
In-app purchases. *See* Apps: In-app purchases	
Input/Output	11
Internet Service Provider	78
iOS 7	11, 14, 38
iPad	
Charging	18
Introduction	8
Simplicity	9
iPad Mini	10
iPad Settings.	See Settings
iPhoto	149

iSight camera	11, 136
iTunes	134
Synchronizing	134
iTunes Radio	135
iTunes Store	134
Ive	
Jonathan	14
iWork	115

K

Kayak	175
Keeping notified	111
Keyboard	
Adding	48
Editing text	53-54
Entering text	52
Formatting text	54
Moving	55-56
Overview	48-49
Selecting text	53
Settings	50-51
Shortcuts	57-59
Deleting	59
Using	59
Splitting	56
Text abbreviations	58
Undocking	55
Keynote	115
Kindle	
On your iPad	130-132
Reading a Kindle book	132

L

Laplication	175
Location Services	21
Locking your iPad	182
Lock screen	
Using	39
London Tube Map	176

M

Magazines	120-121
Mail	82-84
Malware	183
Maps	156-166
Finding contacts	163
Finding locations	158
Flyover	165
Getting directions	160-162
Traffic	164
Types	164-165
Using Pins	159
Viewing	157
McAfee Global Threat Intelligence	183
Mercury Web Browser	102
Messages	88-89
Messaging	
With iMessages	88-89
Meter Readings	186
Mint.com	186
Money	184
Money for iPad Free	186
Multitasking (Multitouching) Gestures	28-31
Moving between open apps	31
Moving between photos	31
Moving items	31
Viewing notifications	31
Multitasking window	16, 24-25
Music	
Buying	134
Playing	135
myLanguage Free Translator	175

N

National Geographic Traveler	175
Newspapers	120-121
Newsstand	120-121
New York Subway Map	175
Notability	114
Notes	
Creating	104-105

O

Notification Center	31, 112
Notifications	111-112
Numbers	115

Online banking	184
On/Off button	12
Opening items	17
Opera Mini Web Browser	102
Operating system	38
Over 40 Magnifier and Flashlight	176

P

Pages	115
Navigating pages	98
Panorama (360)	149
Paris Transport Map	176
PDF	115
Phone calls	
With Skype	90
Photo Booth	146
Photo Collage HD	149
Photos	137-146
Camera Roll	136
Composing with a grid	136
Copying	141, 142
Creating albums	140
Editing	144-145
Enlarging	31
Printing	142
Sharing	142
Special effects	146
Taking	137
Viewing	138
Photo Stream	138
Photo Translator	176
Phrasebook	176
Pictures	
Creating	151
Pictures with Words	92

Pinching   30
Pins.   See Maps: Using Pins
Places To See Before You Die   174
Playable   149
Pocket Expense   186
P&O Cruises   176
Popplet   114
Portable Document Format.   See PDF
PowerCam HD   149
Powerpoint   115
Printing   118
Property
    Viewing   185

R

Rebooting   12
Reminders
    Setting   106-107
Restricting apps   179
Restrictions   178-179
    Passcode   179
Retina Display   11

S

Safari   94-101
    Address Bar   94
    Autofill   96
    Block Cookies   97
    Bookmarking pages   100
    Clear Cookies and Data   97
    Clear History   97
    Do Not Track   97
    Favorites window   99
    Fraud Warning   97
    Navigating pages   98
    New tabs   99
    Pop-up messages   97
    Reader   98
    Reading List   101
    Settings   96
    Shared Links   101

Screen   11
Screenshots   46
Searching for items   34
Sensors   11
Settings   20-21
    Airplane Mode   20
    Bluetooth   20
    Brightness & Wallpaper   21
    Control Center   20
    Do Not Disturb   20
    FaceTime   21
    General   20
    iBooks   21
    iCloud   21
    iTunes & App Stores   21
    Mail, Contacts, Calendars   21
    Maps   21
    Messages   21
    Music   21
    Newsstand   21
    Notes   21
    Notification Center   20
    Photos & Camera   21
    Privacy   21
    Reminders   21
    Safari   21
    Sounds   20
    Videos   21
    Wi-Fi   20
Setting up   13
    Apple ID   13
    Country   13
    Diagnostic information   13
    Find My iPad   13
    iCloud   13
    Language   13
    Location Services   13
    Registering   13
    Wi-Fi   13
SharePrice   186
Sharing   62
Side Switch   12
Siri   16, 32-33
Sixt Rent a Car   176
Skeuomorphic   14
SkyFire Web Browser   102

Skype	90-91
Downloading	90
Using	90-91
Smart Cover	40-41
As a stand	40
Smart Office 2	115
Social networking	
Adding accounts	85
Speaker	12
Specifications	11
Spotlight	
Accessing	34
Search	34-35
Settings	34
Swiping	29

T

Tabbed browsing.	See Safari: New tabs
Talkatone	92
Tapping	29
Text.	See also Keyboard
Insertion point	53
Select All	53
Texting.	See Messaging
Traveling	168-176
Currency	173
Hotels	172
Planning	169-170
Viewing flights	171
TripAdvisor	172
TV and video	
Mirroring	11
Tweeting	142
Twitter	62, 85, 92, 101, 142

U

Unlocking the screen	39
Updating software	38
Urbanspoon	176

V

Video chatting	86
Video Downloader	149
Video Editor for FREE	149
Videos	
Capturing	147
Viewing	148
VIPs.	See Email: VIPs
VirusBarrier	183
Viruses	183
Voice Dictation	60
VoiceOver	42
Voice search	16
Voice typing	60
Volume button	12

W

Wallpapers	
For backgrounds	15
Weather+	176
Web browser.	See Safari
Wi-Fi	78
Wi-Fi Finder	176
Windows Live Hotmail	92
Word	115
WordPress	92
World Calendar	114

Y

Yahoo! Messenger	92
Yelp	176

Z

Zooming	29
By swiping outwards	30